Dr. Seuss Workbook
GRADE 1

Contents

READING

EXPLORE YOUR WORLD!

Throughout this book, you'll find activity pages that encourage kids to learn and explore everywhere. These pages don't follow the specific learning goals of the lessons. They are meant to expand learning beyond the book, sending kids searching, counting, and crafting all around the house—and even outside!

MATH

FEELINGS

SCIENCE

Dear Parents,

There's a world of learning inside the pages of this workbook, and your child will get the most out of it with your support. Here are some tips:

- Encourage your child. Positivity is important, especially when your child finds a task frustrating or difficult!

- Make sure your child has a quiet, comfortable place to work.

- Read the activity directions with your child.

- Give your child a variety of colored pencils and markers to work with.

- Check your child's answers and gently guide your child to the correct response if it wasn't his or her first choice.

- Spend extra time with your child on the areas that he or she finds difficult.

- Pull out your child's best work and display the pages around your home.

- Many of the pages in this book are creative activities that don't have just one right answer. For activities that have specific answers, look for them at the back of this book, starting on page 293.

READING

The more that you **READ**, the more things you'll **KNOW**. The more that you **LEARN**, the more places you'll **GO**.

Get Ready, Readers!

We're learning to read.
We're ready to go.
Let's start by exploring
some sounds we should know.

Trace the trail and say the
words as you pass them.

apple

ball

kite

cake

drum

jam

egg

ink

fish

grape

hat

lion

mitt

nest

owl

pot

queen

rose

top

shoe

umbrella

whisk

vase

xylophone

zipper

yam

7

Jam with Sam

Match each word to the correct picture.

snail

ham

pan

cake

hat

crab

Circle all the words that have the letter A in them.

pine	bat
pan	sat
rug	bin
rake	sun
happy	stare
bite	fine
rate	fun
rot	jog

Words with E in Them

Find a path that only crosses through words with an E in them. Say each word as you pass it.

Write the letter **E** to finish each word. Then read them aloud.

b__an

k__y

qu__en

l__af

sh__ep

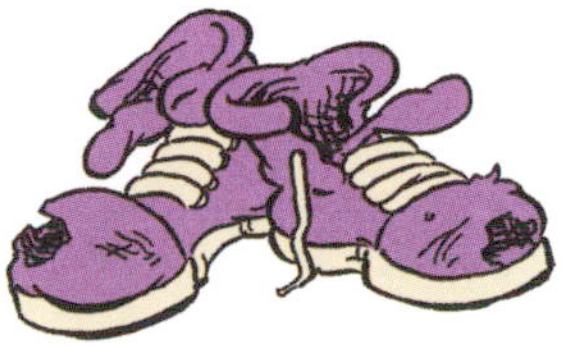

sn__akers

11

Words with I in Them

Circle all the words that are spelled with an I in them.

rug	jig
pig	slide
hit	ride
hot	fish
kind	big
log	dig
wig	pot

Color each thing that has an **I** in its name.

Words with O in Them

Write the letter O to finish each word. Then read them aloud.

bl__ck

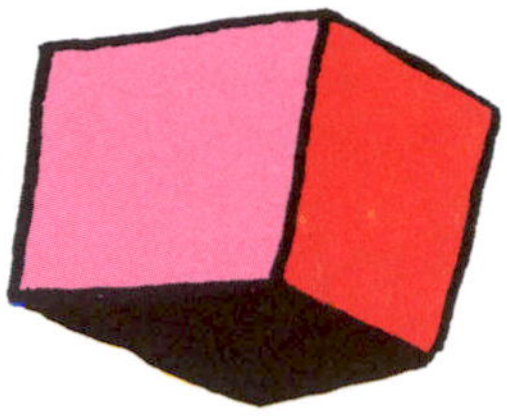

apr__n

b__at

bo__k

c__w

Find a path that only crosses through words with an O.
Say each word as you pass it.

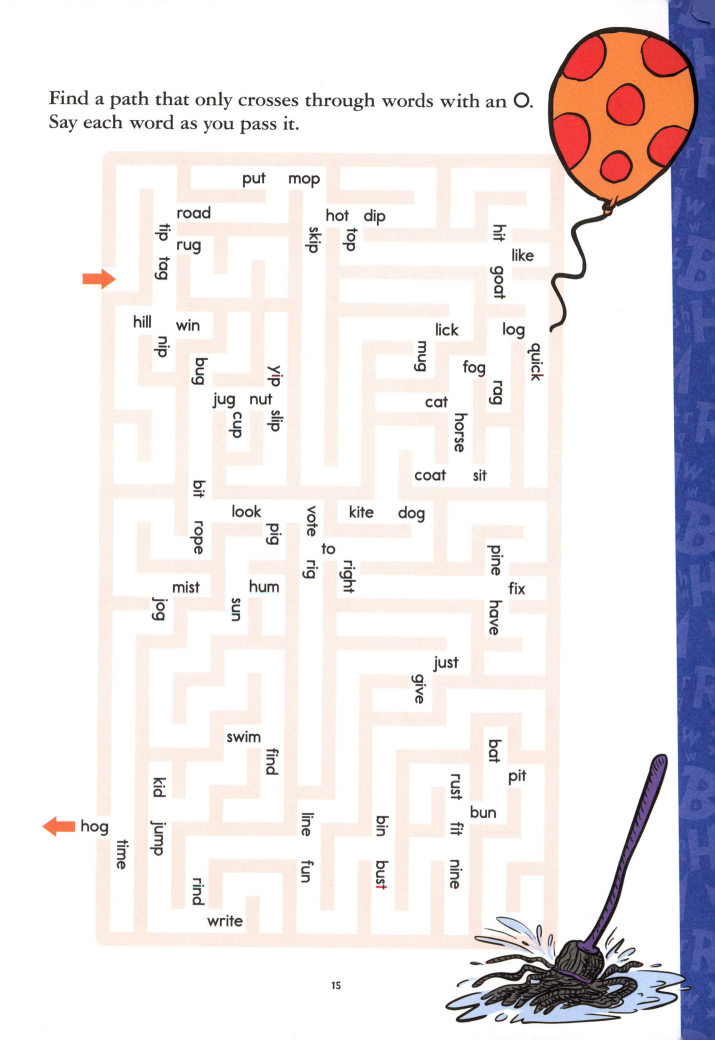

Words with U in Them

Write the letter U to finish each word. Then read them aloud.

co___ch

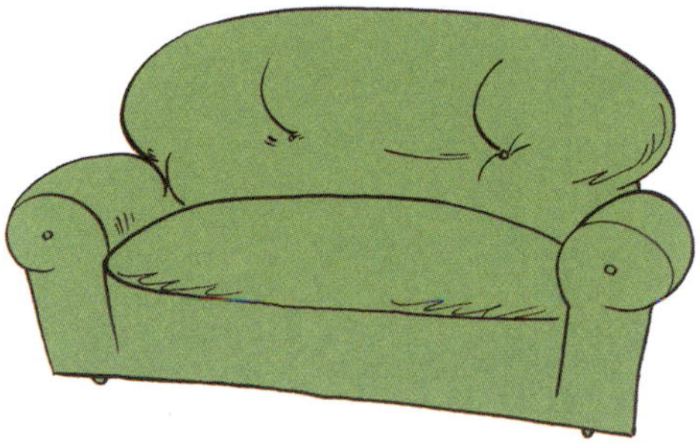

dr___m

d___ck

gl___e

s___n

Circle all the words that are spelled with a U in them.

hog   fun

cut   win

zip   tar

bun   hug

run   fig

hut   dog

pin   cub

rat   sip

Chippity Chop

Circle nine things that end in **-ip**.
Draw a square around nine things that end in **-op**.

chip   hip

sap   flop

chop   clip

flip   wrap

                        slop

                        nap

hop	dip
clop	tip
map	rip
whip	drip
pop	shop
bop	plop

Get Ready, Readers!

YOU DID IT!

Long Vowel Sounds with E & Y

Some words that you read
end with **E** or with **Y**.
They may break the rules—
we can give it a **try**!

Words that **rhyme** have the same ending sound.

Draw a line to connect the words that rhyme.

cake	pride
frame	bake
rose	tame
wave	hose
hide	cave

Find and circle the words that end in E or Y hidden among the letters. Look for them up, down, across, and diagonally. Use the words in the word box to help you.

candy	mane	rate	sky
cane	sunny	July	bunny
try	cute	ripe	baby

H A U K G Q K S E J L

R N Y Z X Y B K G Q R

C A H S U N N Y F D B

V I T A R E V O V F I

M A N E S T G B A B Y

P T N F Q U V W O Q G

W E C U W C J U L Y B

Y N A U R I A T G J U

Q Y N H V I X N O R N

T B E W S P P W D D N

B R E N Z B Y E B Y Y

G I Y N P L V K T I F

The Amazing Letter E

Copy the word from the left to each space on the right. You'll make a new word each time!

can   _____ e

pin   _____ e

cap   _____ e

pan   _____ e

Draw a line to connect the words that rhyme.
Remember: A letter **E** at the end of a word changes the sound of other vowels.

win	bit
kite	cube
car	cub
tub	bar
fine	fin
kit	mine
care	bare
tube	bite

Hooray for the Letter E!

Unscramble each set of letters to spell words that end in E. Use the words in the word box to help you.

fire	care	bone	fuse

_____

r c a e

_____

e o b n

_____

r e f i

_____

s f e u

Circle all the pictures with names that end in **E**.

Ending in Y

Circle all the pictures with names that end in Y.

Find a path that only crosses through words ending in Y.

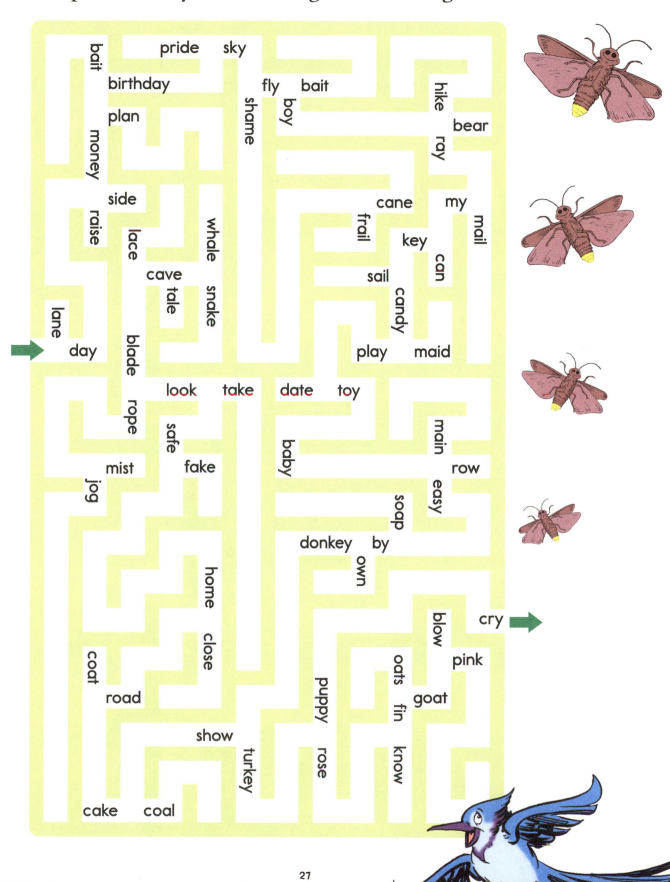

bait
pride   sky
birthday   fly   bait   hike
plan   shame   boy   ray   bear
money   cane   my   mail
side   frail   key   can
raise   whale   sail
lace   cave   snake   candy   mail
tale   play   maid
lane
day   blade   look   take   date   toy
rope   safe   main   row
mist   fake   baby   easy
jog   soap
donkey   by
own
blow   cry
home   pink
coat   close   oats   fin   goat
road   puppy   rose   know
show
turkey
cake   coal

Letter E Strikes Again!

Read each word aloud. Then color the E at the end to make a new word and read it aloud again. How did it change?

can e

quit e

do e

at e

pine

site

dine

tube

Sight Words

Here are some special sight words.
You'll see them every day.
And once you've learned them,
you can shout,
"I'm reading! Hip, hooray!"

Let's start with the shortest words. Can you recognize them? Read them aloud as you go.

A	as	by	he
am	at	do	I
an	be	go	if

Write a sentence using as many of these sight words as you can.

_____

_____

_____

Try these sight words now.

in	my	on	to
is	no	or	up
it	of	so	we

Write a sentence using as many of these sight words as you can.

_____

_____

_____

Coloring Sight Words

Read and color these sight words.

come

with

been

into

for out
him see
find

Counting Syllables

A **syllable** is a beat in a word.

Man has one syllable.
Many has two.

Say each sight word slowly and count the number of beats.

about	follow
come	number
first	other
many	one
from	people
water	said
word	the
mother	these

Write the words that had one syllable in the green box.
Write the words that had two syllables in the orange box.

one syllable	two syllables
_____	_____
_____	_____
_____	_____
_____	_____
_____	_____
_____	_____
_____	_____
_____	_____

More Sight Words

Read and color these sight words.

each all
then and
down

part

made

day / she

but

Sight Words

YOU DID IT!

tap
and
pie

pen
eat
run
lip

ink
ear
win

to
if
is

Words in Words

Look at the pages with short words on the left.
Can you find those words inside the longer
words on the right?

Now let's go on a hidden-word hunt. Look
around your home and search for long words
that have shorter words inside them. Look in
books, on boxes, and on posters, too.

Vowel Teams

Let's practice our vowels—
you don't have to ask twice.
There's a short **I** in **him**
and a long **I** in **nice**!

When vowels team up,
they make sounds that are new.
Like the **AI** in **rain**
or the **UE** in **blue**.

Let's review some vowel sounds. Sort the **long vowel** words and **short vowel** words, then write them in the correct box.

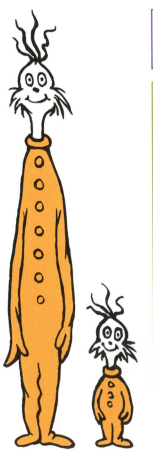

fruit	fun	ball	net	pot
bit	nail	keep	coat	bike

long vowels	short vowels
_____	_____
_____	_____
_____	_____
_____	_____
_____	_____

Color the pictures with names that have long vowel sounds blue.
Color the pictures with names that have short vowel sounds red.

41

Long A Pairs

Circle the words that have a long A sound made by **AI**. Draw a rectangle around the words where **AY** makes the long A sound.

rain	say
day	tray
play	wait
stay	tail
pain	pay
main	clay
mail	bait

Color the words that have a long A sound in them.

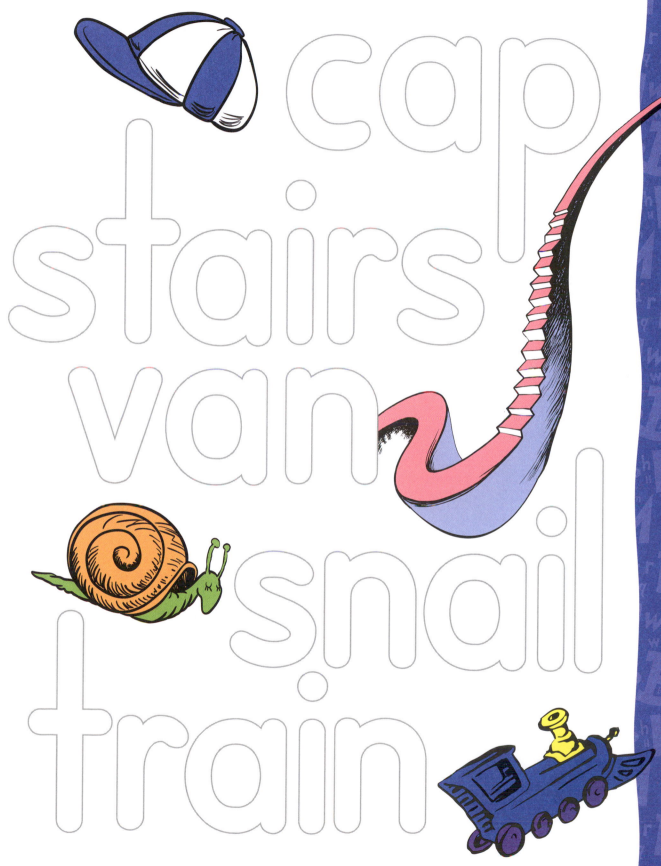

cap

stairs

van

snail

train

Long E Pairs

Circle the words that have a long E sound made by EE.
Put a box around the words where EY makes the long E sound.

chimney	deer
hockey	feet
key	freeze
meet	green
donkey	knee
queen	need
free	valley

Complete each word with either **EE** or **EY**.

monk_____

tr_____

thr_____

ch____se

mon_____

b_____

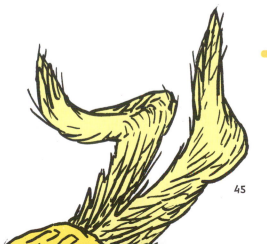

hon_____

f____t

45

Long O Pairs

Circle the words that have a long O sound made by OA.
Put a box around the words where OE makes the O sound.

boat   road

coat   soap

toe   goal

coal   foe

hoe   soak

goat   loan

doe   woe

Write the long O words next to each picture.

_____

_____

_____

AU and AW

Read each word aloud.
Copy the words with AU into the AU box.
Copy the words with AW into the AW box.

auto   hawk   sauce

paw   laws   caution

straw   cause   lawn

AU	AW
_____	_____
_____	_____
_____	_____
_____	_____
_____	_____

48

Color the words with **AU** blue.
Color the words with **AW** green.

jaw
vault
yawn
saw
pause

E Vowel Combinations

IE makes a long **I** sound. Write **IE** to complete each word.

p_____

tr_____s

t_____

fr_____s

l_____

fl_____s

UE makes a long U sound. Write UE to complete each word.

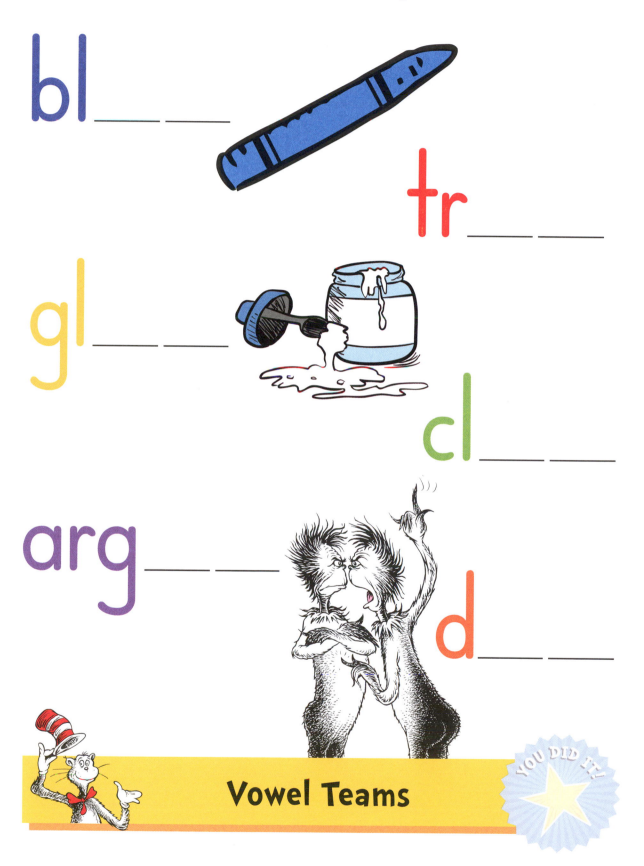

bl_____

tr_____

gl_____

cl_____

arg_____

d_____

Vowel Teams

YOU DID IT!

51

Hardworking Letters

Some powered-up letters make more than one sound. The letters O, C, and G are the hardest workers around!

Read each word aloud.
Sort them by the sound OO makes.

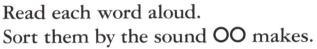

look	cook	hook	room	too
took	good	roof	moo	pool

OO as in "moon"

_____

_____

_____

_____

_____

OO as in "book"

_____

_____

_____

_____

_____

Write down as many OO words as you can think of.

_____

_____

_____   _____

_____   _____

_____   _____

_____   _____

_____   _____

_____   _____

O Pairs

OW can make two sounds. One of them is the same sound as OU.

Read the words aloud and copy them.

flower _____

south _____

house _____

tower _____

mouse _____

cow _____

couch _____

OW can also make a long O sound. Let's compare the two OW sounds.

Read each word aloud. Sort them by the sound OW makes.

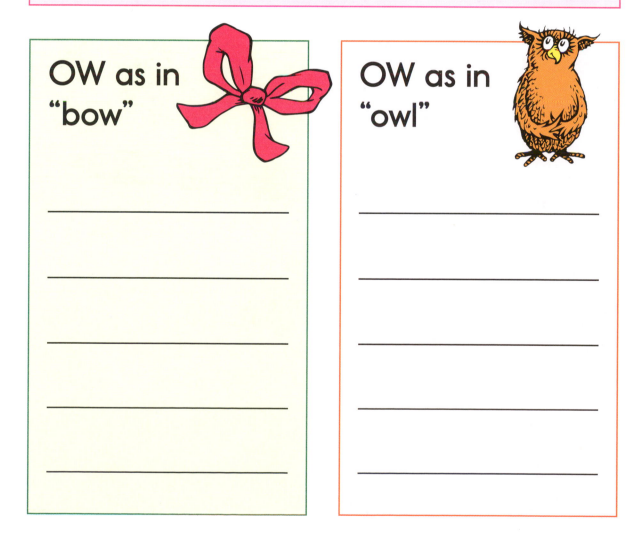

glow   clown   snow

towel   brown   grow

power   shower   flow

OW as in "bow"

_____

_____

_____

_____

_____

OW as in "owl"

_____

_____

_____

_____

_____

Hard and Soft C

When C comes before A, O, or U, it makes a K sound. This is a **hard** C.
When C comes before E, I, or Y, it makes an S sound. This is a **soft** C.

Say the name of each picture. Circle the pictures with names that
make an S sound. Draw a rectangle around the ones that make a
K sound. *Hint:* The sound you are looking for might not be at the
start of the word.

Write the word that has both a hard and a soft C.

—— —— —— —— —— ——

Read each word aloud. If the C makes a K sound, color it blue.
If the C makes an S sound, color it red.

cup

rice

face

coin

ice

Hard and Soft G

The letter **G** makes two sounds, too. It can sound hard, as in **grape**, or it can sound soft, as in **germ**.

Say the name of each picture. Circle the pictures with names that make a hard **G** sound. Draw a rectangle around the ones that make a soft **G** sound.

Write the word that has both a hard and a soft **G**.

——— —— —— —— ——   —— —— ——

Read each G word aloud. Write the word in green if it has a hard G sound. Write the word in yellow if it has a soft G sound.

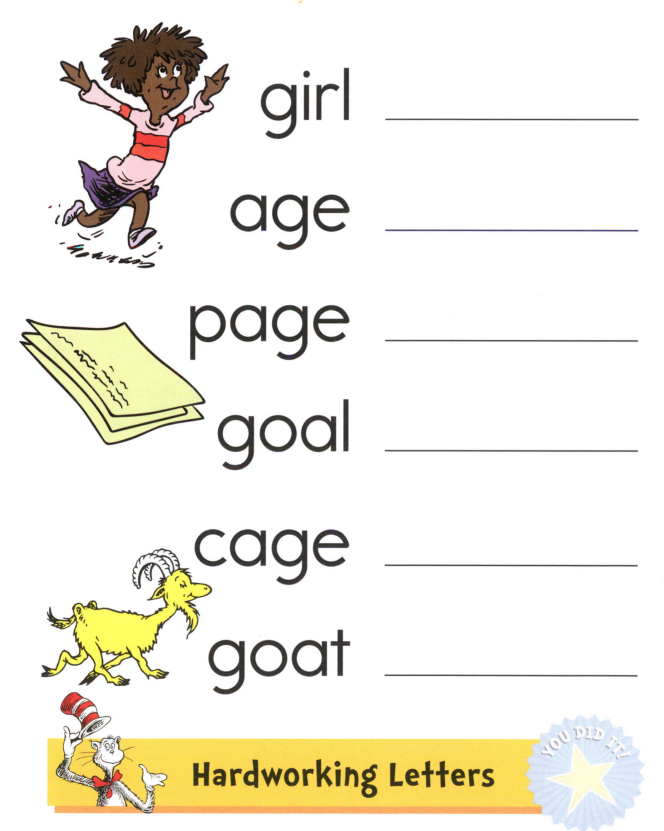

girl _____

age _____

page _____

goal _____

cage _____

goat _____

Hardworking Letters

YOU DID IT!

Consonant Blends

When consonants combine to make sounds,
those letters form a **blend**.
They can show up anyplace in a word—
the beginning, middle, or end.

Put an X in the box next to the blend that is found in each word.

☐ bl   ☐ sl
☐ fl   ☐ cl

☐ bl   ☐ sl
☐ fl   ☐ cl

☐ bl   ☐ sl
☐ fl   ☐ cl

☐ bl   ☐ sl
☐ fl   ☐ cl

Write the correct blend to complete each word.

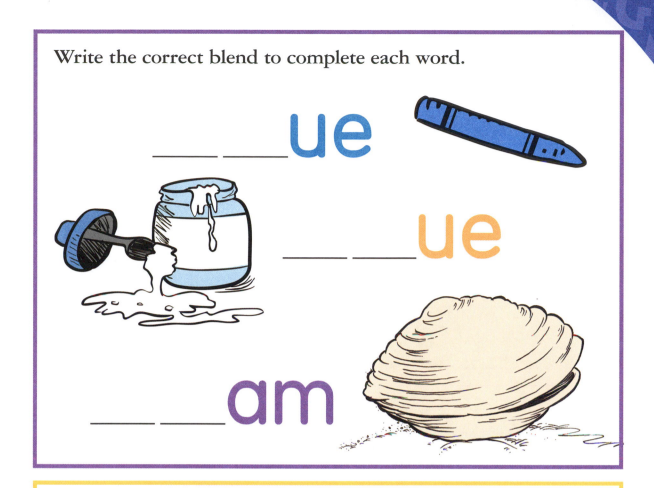

_____ _____ue

_____ _____ue

_____ _____am

Read and copy these words with consonant blends.

play _____

flap _____

clay _____

slip _____

R Blends

These words are missing their beginning letters. Write in the R blend to complete each word. Use the letters in the box to help you.

cr	fr	pr	tr	gr

_____ee

_____een

_____own

_____og

_____esent

Circle the **R** blend that appears in the name of each object.

tr / dr

gr / tr

gr / br

dr / fr

br / cr

gr / br

S Blends

These words are missing their beginning letters. Write in the S blend to complete each word. Use the letters in the box to help you.

sl	sp	st	sw	sm

_____op

_____oon

_____ug

_____eet

_____ile

Some **S** blends have three letters.

Put an X in the box next to the blend that is found in each word.

☐ sl   ☐ scr
☐ squ   ☐ str

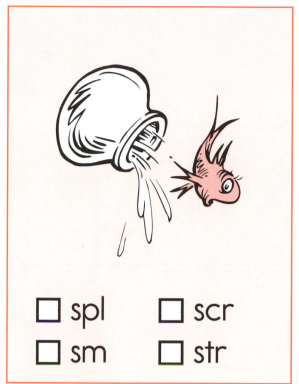

☐ spl   ☐ scr
☐ sm   ☐ str

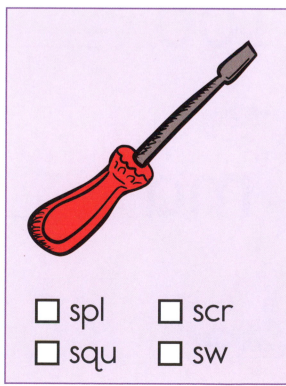

☐ spl   ☐ scr
☐ squ   ☐ sw

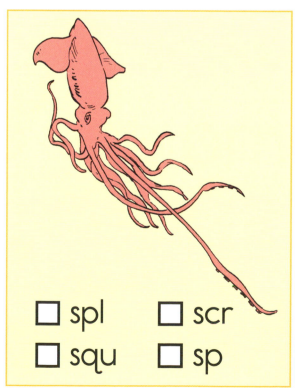

☐ spl   ☐ scr
☐ squ   ☐ sp

T Blends

Add **TH** to complete each word.

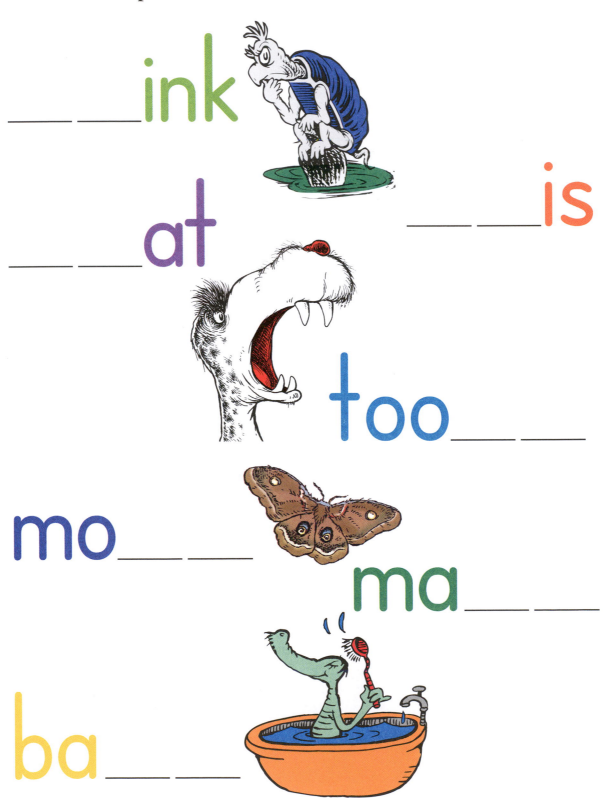

_____ink

_____at

_____is

too_____

mo_____

ma_____

ba_____

Find a path that only goes through the things that have TR.

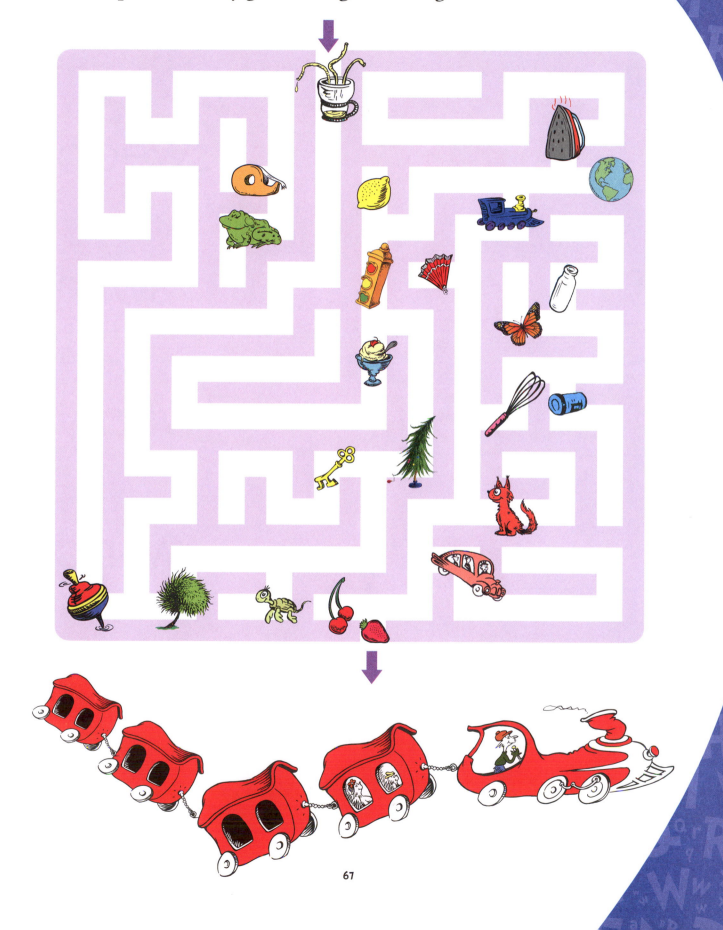

67

W Blends

Add **SW** or **TW** to complete each word.
Then draw a line to match it to the complete word.

_____eet   sweep

_____in   swim

_____im   twenty

_____enty   swing

_____eep   sweet

_____ing   twin

Circle the words that begin with a consonant blend.

flip   three   plate

clip   tree   free

cat   tap   drum

blue   cake   saw

Write the words you circled.

_____   _____

_____   _____

_____   _____

_____   _____

End Blends

Blends can be found at the end of a word, too.

Add **ND** or **MP** to complete the word for each picture.

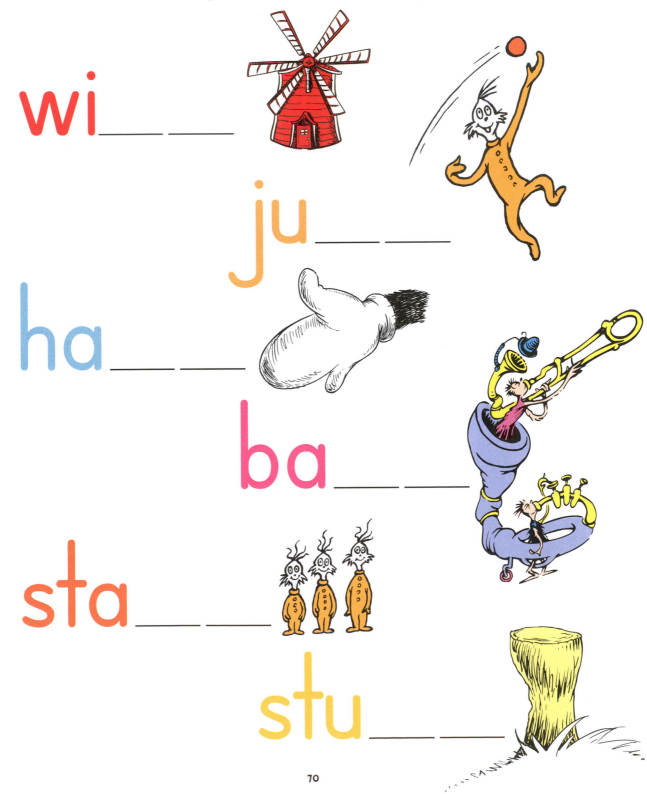

wi_____

ju_____

ha_____

ba_____

sta_____

stu_____

70

Complete the words. Use clues from the sentences to figure out which word is correct. Use the letters in the box to help you.

rd	rt	rm	rn	rp

I can't wait for school to sta____.

The tree blew over in the sto____.

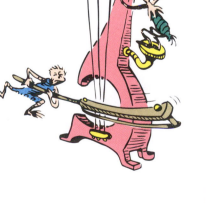

It was not very ha____ to find you over there.

You play that song on the ha____ very well.

The animals are safe in the ba____.

End Blends with L and N

Put an X in the box next to the blend that is found at the end of the name for each picture.

☐ nk   ☐ lt

☐ lt   ☐ lk

☐ lk   ☐ st

☐ st   ☐ nk

Circle the words that end with a consonant blend.

act　　　melt　　　best

fact　　　bed　　　pool

face　　　link　　　cart

card　　　most　　　feel

Write the words you circled.

_____　　　_____

_____　　　_____

_____　　　_____

_____　　　_____

Consonant Blends

Words with Three Consonants and One Vowel

First we read words with three letters.
Next up is words with four.
Soon you'll be reading words
 with many, many more!

Write the name of each animal below its picture.

_____

_____

_____

_____

Mix and Match the word beginnings and endings to make new words. Put the words that make sense in the **real** column. Put the nonsense words in the **silly** column.

beginnings	TH	CH	SH	
endings	IN	IP	OP	UT

real	silly
_____	_____
_____	_____
_____	_____
_____	_____
_____	_____
_____	_____
_____	_____

CVCC Words

These pages have words that begin with
a consonant, then a vowel, followed by two more consonants.

Circle the word that matches the picture.

set   nest

net   nets

lamp   lime

camp   tame

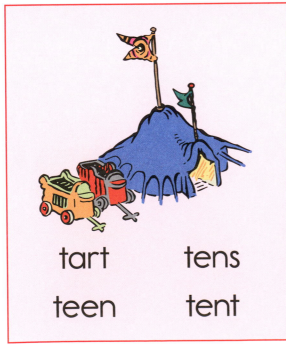

tart   tens

teen   tent

belt   bell

bent   labs

Read each word and draw a picture of it.

desk

fish

sink

king

77

CCVC Words

These pages have words that begin with two consonants, then a vowel, followed by one more consonant.

Circle the word that matches the picture.

frog   fast

lime   fin

crab   bark

crib   cars

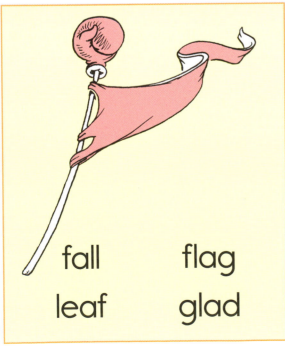

fall   flag

leaf   glad

leak   kale

slip   keel

Read each word and draw a picture of it.

drum

clap

swam

star

Powerful Pairs

Circle the CCVC or CVCC word that matches the picture.

slip
swim
seal

clam
climb
crib

vine
vest
vast

ship
shop
flip

pack
plum
pick

fire
four
fork

Read and copy each word.

salt _____

skip _____

link _____

slip _____

cart _____

hawk _____

flip _____

desk _____

Words with Three Consonants and One Vowel

YOU DID IT!

Rhyme Time

Can you find two things here with names that rhyme with **fox**? Then try to spot things that rhyme with **chicks**.

Now go take the time to rhyme!

Search your home or go outside and try to find five different pairs of things that rhyme. Will you see a bee near a tree? Is there a can and a pan?

Good luck!

Parts of Speech

Have you heard about **verbs**?
Do you know about **nouns**?

They are some of the best
parts of speech that I've found!

Different types of words are known as
parts of speech.

Draw a line to match each word with its definition.

noun

a word that can be used to replace a noun

verb

a word that describes something

adjective

a person, place, or thing

pronoun

an action word

Use one noun and one verb from each box to write a sentence.

nouns	verbs
boy dog	eats plays
girl cat	sings holds

_____

_____

Draw a picture that shows what your sentence is about.

Nouns

Underline the noun in each sentence.
The first one has been done to show you how.

John is sad.

Anika is sewing.

Mr. Brown can moo.

The dog barks.

The car is fast.

Mr. Knox stands in the box.

Thing 1 likes oranges.

Jim is a runner.

Circle the words that are nouns.

go   pig   bite

boy   ride   tree

fox   bike   hop

man   bake   rug

Write the words you circled.

_____   _____

_____   _____

_____   _____

_____   _____

Verbs

Circle the words that are verbs.

cry   cookie

walk   sit

skip   sad

hot   apple

Choose one verb that you circled. Draw a picture showing that action.

Find and circle the verbs hidden among the letters.
Look for them up, down, across, and diagonally.
Use the words in the word box to help you.

run	eat	ski	read
jump	hide	clap	draw
play	ride	swim	nap

Y L U R M G I Y P V T

S D J I E S H J U M P

E L W D M Y I Z I Q V

A S I D K R P C E C B

T H X D U Y A L B K H

R G U O R U N A A D R

R E A D G A D P H Y G

I X L J C Q W E U O N

L M B B D N O U P S N

R I D E M W S R A Q P

V N O B R Y W K N Y C

F X O W C T P Q I V B

Adjectives

An **adjective** describes something.

Circle the words that are **adjectives**.

cat   run

sad   slide

blue   angry

ham   fish

hot   big

cold   apple

wet   hairy

Find and circle the adjectives hidden among the letters.
Look for them up, down, across, and diagonally.
Use the words in the word box to help you.

happy	fun	tall	kind
clean	big	short	silly
red	small	good	wild

H T R R Q N I Y S D R

P A A Y W A J F M N Q

G L P L V E S O A I L

L O I P L L P D L K P

T X O Z Y C E Y L F J

E C U D Q R L C J M X

O R V Y I L B U H U W

W I L D I R D I I S A

G O A S Z O L M G Y Q

G P M F S C Z P I E N

H V Z C J Q S H O R T

N O R S G F U N F F G

Pronouns

A **pronoun** is a word that replaces a noun.

Circle the **pronoun** that correctly finishes each sentence.

(I / Me) see a bee.

(Us / We) ride our bikes.

What time will (you / us) go home?

(They / Them) went up a tree.

He stamped (his / him) feet on the ground.

(She / Her) used the paint.

Fill in each blank with a pronoun that could replace each noun in red.

Sally (_____) likes to play.

The farmer has to feed **the chickens** (_____) .

Thing 1 and Thing 2 (_____) go down the slide.

I hope **that boy** (_____) will not fall.

Capitalization and Punctuation

Words start with a **capital** letter at the beginning of a sentence or when they are a name. Your name starts with a capital letter, too.

Write one capitalized word for each category.

Your name:

_____

A day of the week:

_____

The month you were born:

_____

Your favorite holiday:

_____

The state you live in:

_____

Punctuation marks help you understand how to say the sentence.

Add either !, ?, or . to finish each sentence.

Did you eat that cookie ___

How are you feeling ___

Go away___

He likes to run ___

I am sad ___

What is your name ___

Hooray___

Parts of Speech

YOU DID IT!

Reading Comprehension

Comprehension is
the skill you need
to understand
the words you read.

Write the answer to each question.

What is the title of a book you like?

_____

What is the story about?

_____

_____

_____

Who are the characters in the story?

_____

Where does the story take place?

_____

What happens at the end?

_____

_____

Draw a picture of something that happens in the story you
just described.

Following Directions

Follow the directions.

1. Read all the directions before you start.
2. Draw a big circle.
3. Draw a triangle.
4. Draw a square.
5. Draw two lines next to each other.
6. Make a picture using the shapes and lines listed above.

Follow the directions. Color the squares as you pass them.

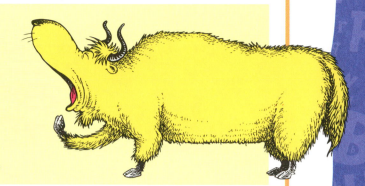

1. Start where it says "start."
2. Move right three squares.
3. Go down two squares.
4. Move right three squares.
5. Move down three squares.

START					

Where did the directions lead you?

_____

Categories

Write each word in the correct box.

plane

bike

apple

spoon

carrot

car

fork

egg

plate

things you can eat	things you can eat with	things you can ride
_____	_____	_____
_____	_____	_____
_____	_____	_____

Circle the characters who are doing something active.
Draw a triangle around the ones who are eating something.
Draw a rectangle around the ones who look happy.

How many characters have both a circle and a rectangle around them?

_____

How many characters do not have a circle, a triangle, or a rectangle around them?

_____

Making Predictions

For each picture, write what you think might happen next.

Real or Imagined?

A sentence which states something that's true is a **fact**. Something you believe or feel is an **opinion**.

Circle whether each sentence is a **fact** or an **opinion**.

She has a blue dress.   fact   opinion

This cake is the best!   fact   opinion

The flower smells bad.   fact   opinion

I ate a red apple.   fact   opinion

It is 30 degrees today!   fact   opinion

They are running.   fact   opinion

The Grinch has a very creepy smile.   fact   opinion

Nonfiction writing is about real people, places, events, or things. **Fiction** is a story that is made up.

Draw a line to match the type of writing to the description.

a talking dog
saves the day

fiction

what I saw
on my way
to school

a family of
monsters lives
under the bed

nonfiction

how to plant
a backyard
garden

Reading Comprehension

YOU DID IT!

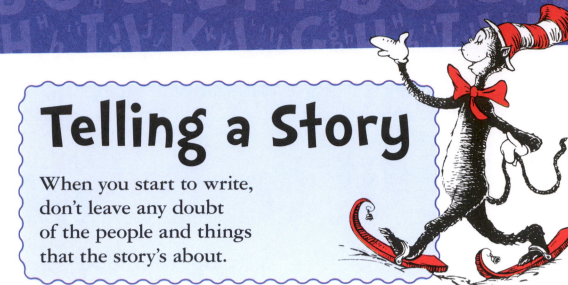

Telling a Story

When you start to write, don't leave any doubt of the people and things that the story's about.

CAT

Who's doing what? Write each character's name on the correct line.

MARVIN

_____ sleeps

_____ falls

ALICE

_____ eats

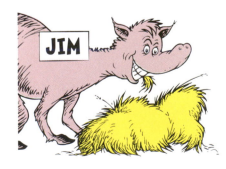

JIM

_____ rides

Unscramble the sentences and rewrite them so that they make sense.

the bed. sleeps He in

_____

ice cream. loves He

_____

the flower. She smells

_____

She car. the drives

_____

Elements of a Story

A story has a **beginning**, a **middle**, and an **end**.

Make up a story about the picture.

Once upon a time _____

_____

_____.

The problem was _____

_____.

The problem was solved by _____

_____.

Draw a picture that shows how the story ends.

Using Descriptive Language

Imagine the best vacation ever. Write about it. Where is it located? What is the weather like? What would you see and do?

_____

_____

_____

_____

_____

_____

_____

_____

_____

_____

Draw a picture of yourself enjoying the vacation to go along with your story.

Adding Detail

Describe the best day you can remember.

Where were you?

_____

When did it happen?

_____

Who was with you?

_____

What was the best part about your day?

_____

_____

_____

How does thinking about that day make you feel?

_____

Use the details you remembered to write about your day.
Use at least four sentences to tell the story.

_____

_____

_____

_____

_____

_____

_____

_____

Name your story: _____

Telling a Story

YOU DID IT!

Tell the Tooth

How many teeth does this big beast have?

Now it's tooth time! Do you have all your teeth?
Count them, and write down how many you have.

Now add your family's number of teeth! How many
total teeth are there in your house? More than 100?

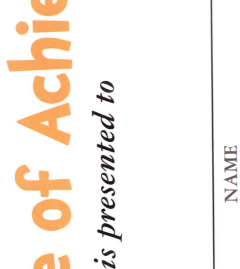

Certificate of Achievement

is presented to

_____

NAME

for becoming a

Remarkable Reader!

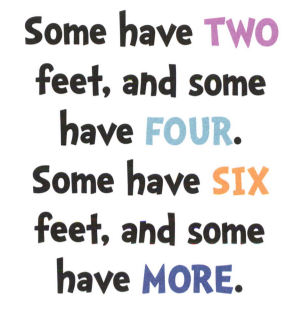

Some have **TWO** feet, and some have **FOUR**. Some have **SIX** feet, and some have **MORE**.

Numbers and Place Value

Numbers are very
important to know.
Let's count up to fifty.
Get ready, set, go!

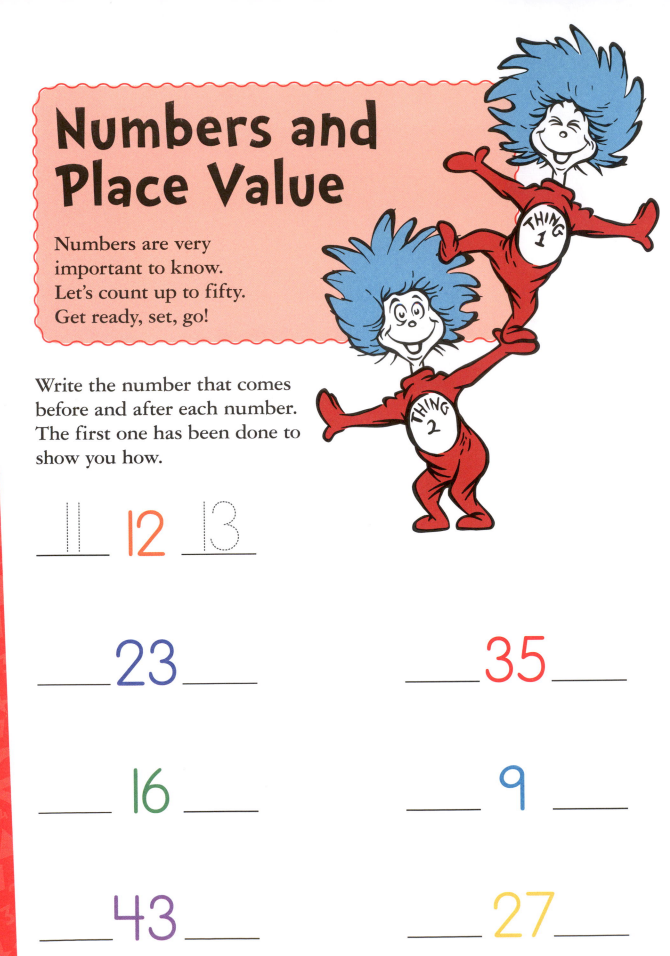

Write the number that comes
before and after each number.
The first one has been done to
show you how.

_11_ 12 _13_

___ 23 ___

___ 35 ___

___ 16 ___

___ 9 ___

___ 43 ___

___ 27 ___

Fill in all the missing
numbers on this trail.

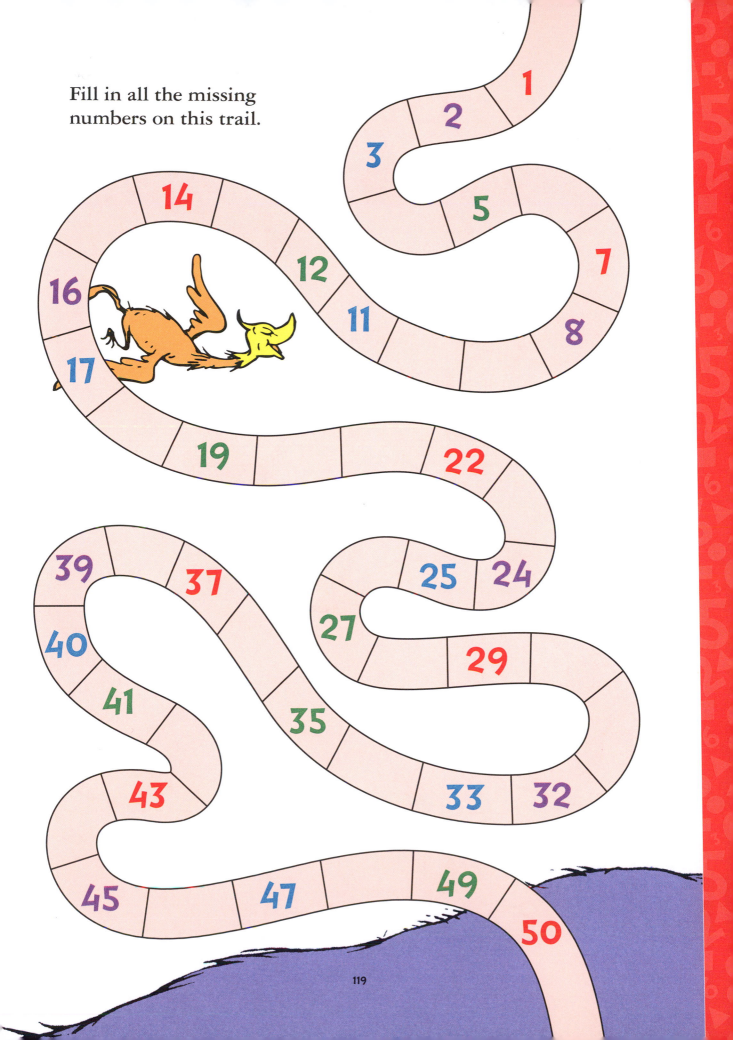

1
2
3
5
7
8
11
12
14
16
17
19
22
24
25
27
29
32
33
35
37
39
40
41
43
45
47
49
50

119

Numbers 1 to 10

Write the number of fish for each dish.

Write the number of stars in each group.

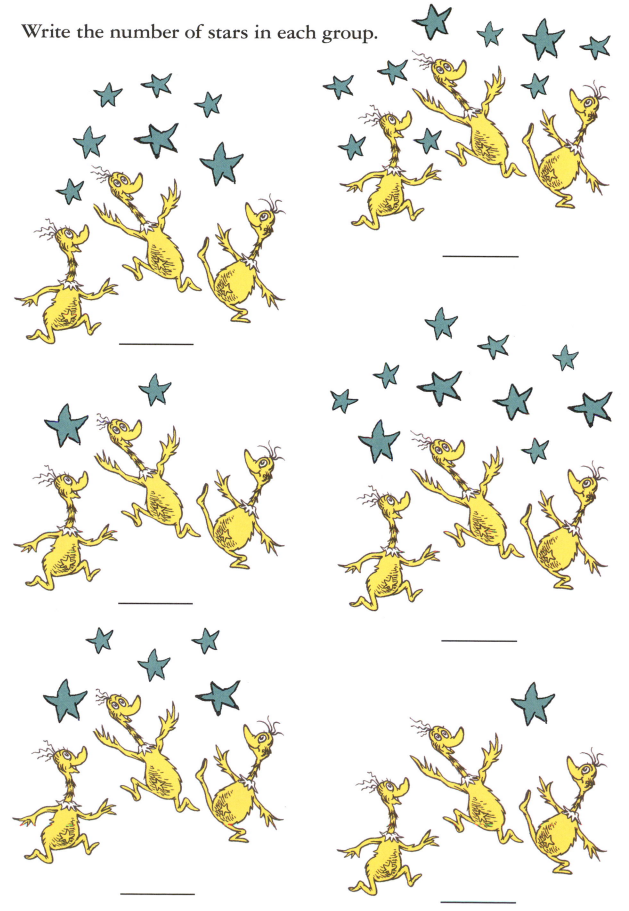

_____

_____

_____

_____

_____

_____

Numbers 11 to 20

Draw a line from each crate to the matching number of items.

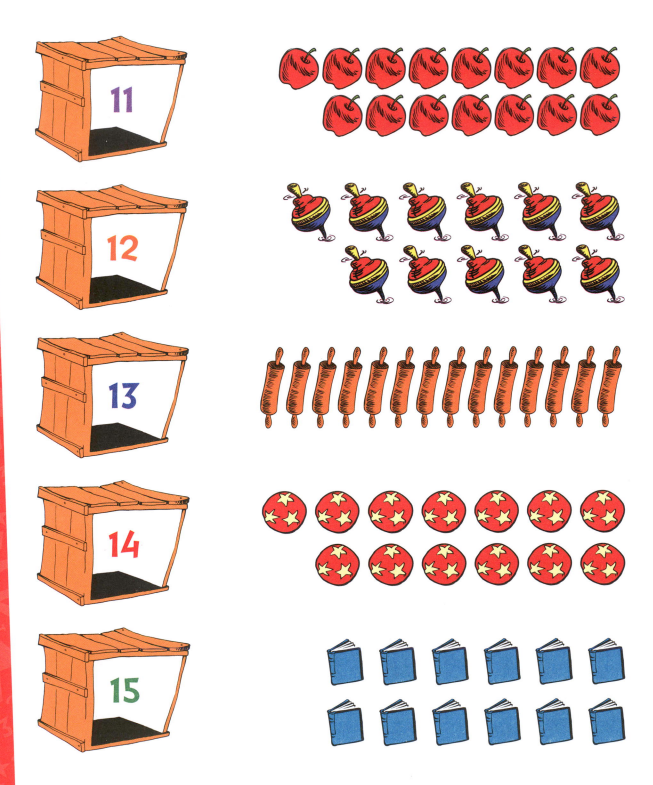

 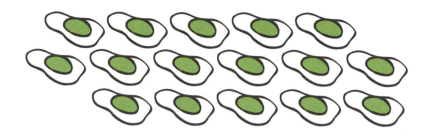

Numbers 21 to 30

Circle 23 birds.

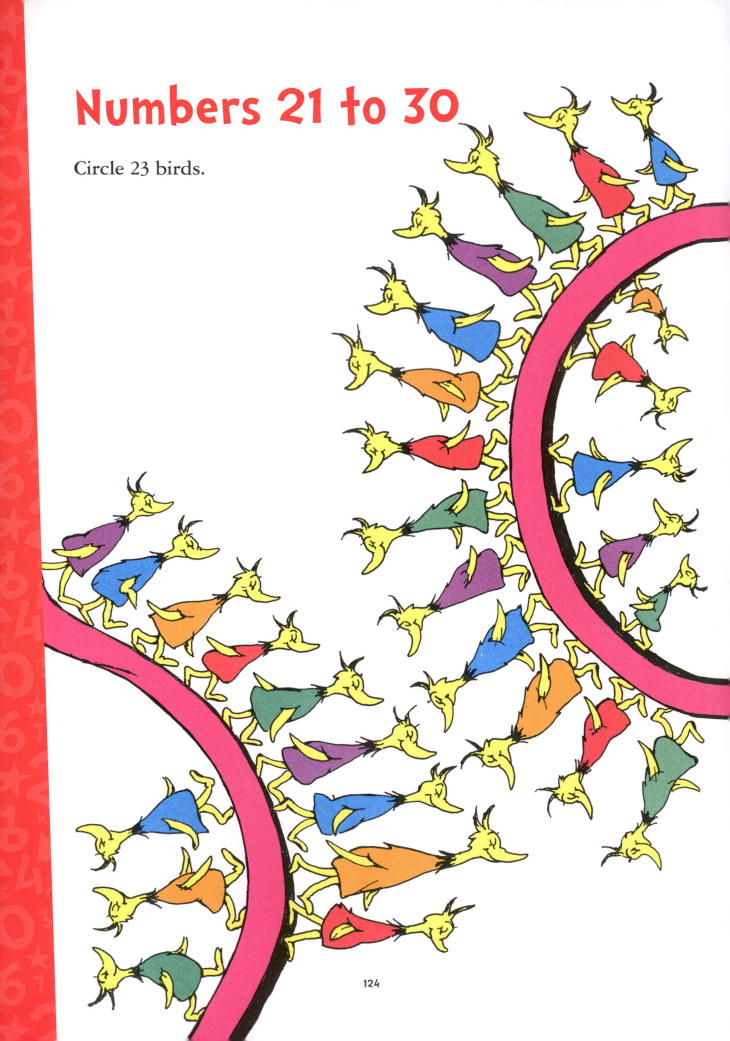

Connect the dots from 1 to 30.

Larger Numbers

Write the number that comes before and after each one.
The first one has been done to show you how.

22 23 24 ___ 75 ___

___ 31 ___ ___ 102 ___

___ 55 ___ ___ 68 ___

___ 96 ___ ___ 114 ___

___ 62 ___ ___ 47 ___

___ 89 ___ ___ 119 ___

Fill in all the missing numbers on this grid.

1		3		5	6		8		10
11	12			15		17			20
	22	23			26		28		30
31			34	35		37			40
	42		44		46		48	49	
51	52			55		57		59	
61			64	65		67			70
	72	73			76		78		
81				85	86		88		90
	92	93			96		98		100
101			104	105		107			
	112			115			118		120

Big Numbers

Write the number of spots that are on each giraffe.

_____ spots

_____ spots

_____ spots

Connect the dots from 1 to 120.

Place Value

When you have a two-digit number, the digit on the left tells you how many tens there are. The digit on the right tells you how many ones there are. That's **place value!**

Write the place values for each number.

21
Tens: _____
Ones: _____

99
Tens: _____
Ones: _____

37
Tens: _____
Ones: _____

43
Tens: _____
Ones: _____

88
Tens: _____
Ones: _____

19
Tens: _____
Ones: _____

56
Tens: _____
Ones: _____

72
Tens: _____
Ones: _____

Look at the bundles of balloons, then write how many tens and ones they each have.

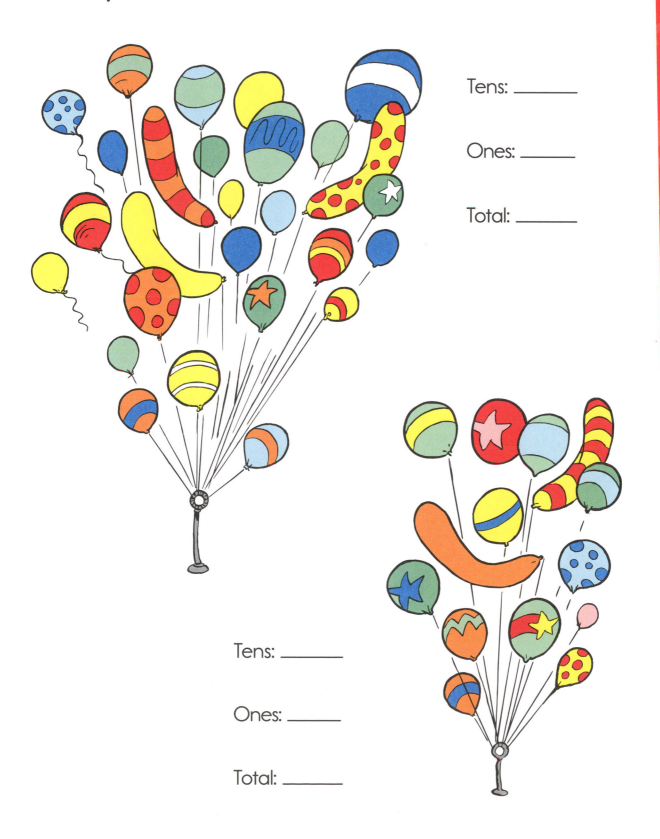

Tens: _____

Ones: _____

Total: _____

Tens: _____

Ones: _____

Total: _____

Place Value to Hundreds

Write the number of hundreds, tens, and ones under each number.

231

Hundreds: _____

Tens: _____

Ones: _____

189

Hundreds: _____

Tens: _____

Ones: _____

743

Hundreds: _____

Tens: _____

Ones: _____

328

Hundreds: _____

Tens: _____

Ones: _____

564

Hundreds: _____

Tens: _____

Ones: _____

936

Hundreds: _____

Tens: _____

Ones: _____

Numbers and Place Value

YOU DID IT!

133

On Your Mark

Read these two sentences out loud:
    I see a fish!
    I see...a fish?

Now try it with other things in your house.
Find some books, boxes, or posters and pick
some sentences to read. Then, read them again
as if they had different punctuation marks.

    It's easy and fun? No.
    It's easy and fun!

Skip Counting

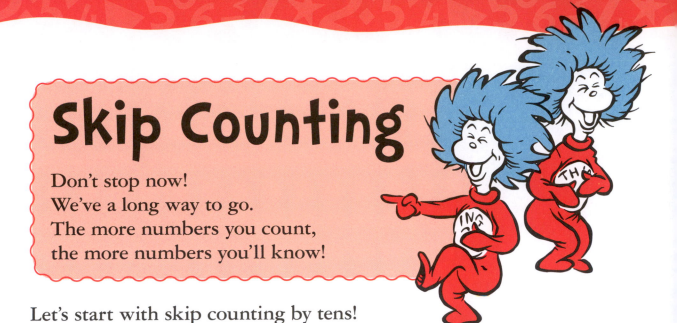

Don't stop now!
We've a long way to go.
The more numbers you count,
the more numbers you'll know!

Let's start with skip counting by tens!

How many dots are in each of these trails? Count by tens and write the number at the finish line of each one. The first one has been done to show you how.

40 dots

_____ dots

FINISH LINE

Skip Counting by Fives

How many books are in each of these bookcases?
Count by fives and write the number next to each one.

_____ books

_____ books

_____ books

How many red clocks do you see? How many blue clocks?
Count by fives and write the number of each.

_____ red clocks

_____ blue clocks

Skip Counting by Twos

Skip counting is when you count up by two, three, four, or more and skip numbers in between.

Count by two! **Two, four, six, eight, ten,** and keep going. When you reach the end, write the total. The first one has been done to show you how.

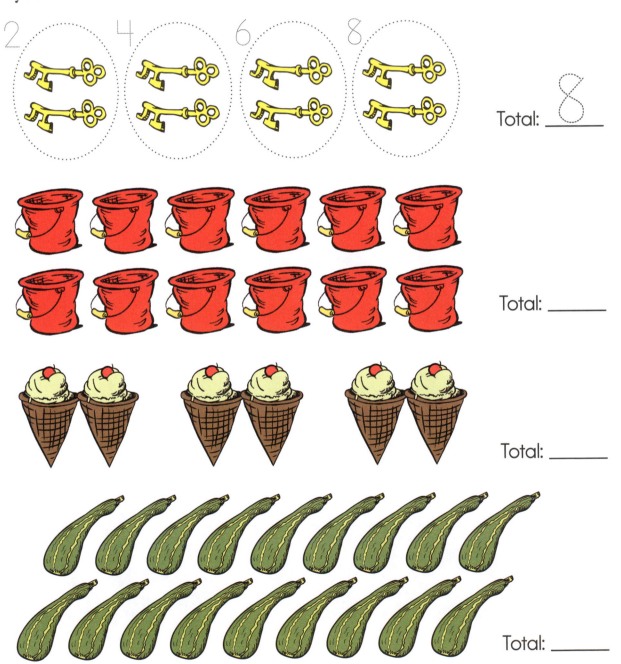

Total: 8

Total: _____

Total: _____

Total: _____

Total: _____

Total: _____

Total: _____

Total: _____

Total: _____

Skip Counting by Threes

Count by threes and write the number of things for each group.
The first one has been done to show you how.

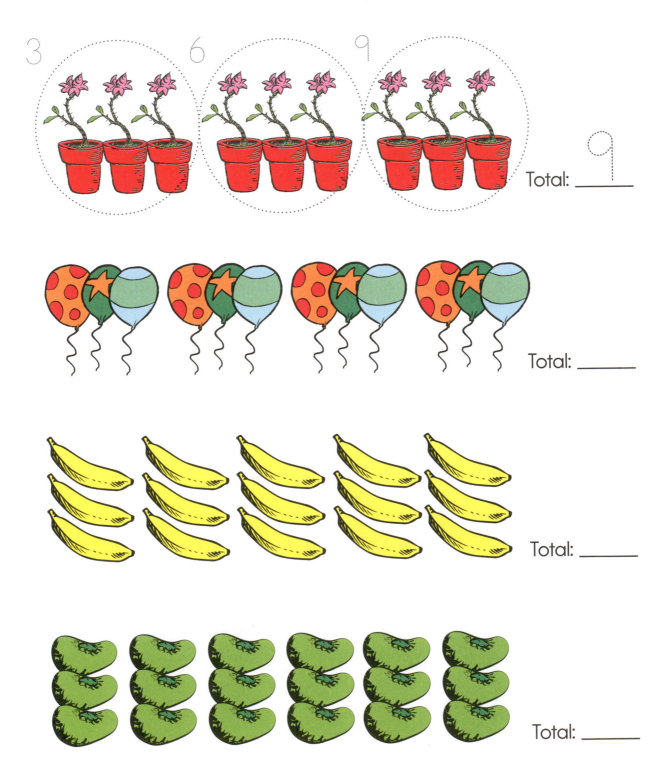

3   6   9   Total: 9

Total: _____

Total: _____

Total: _____

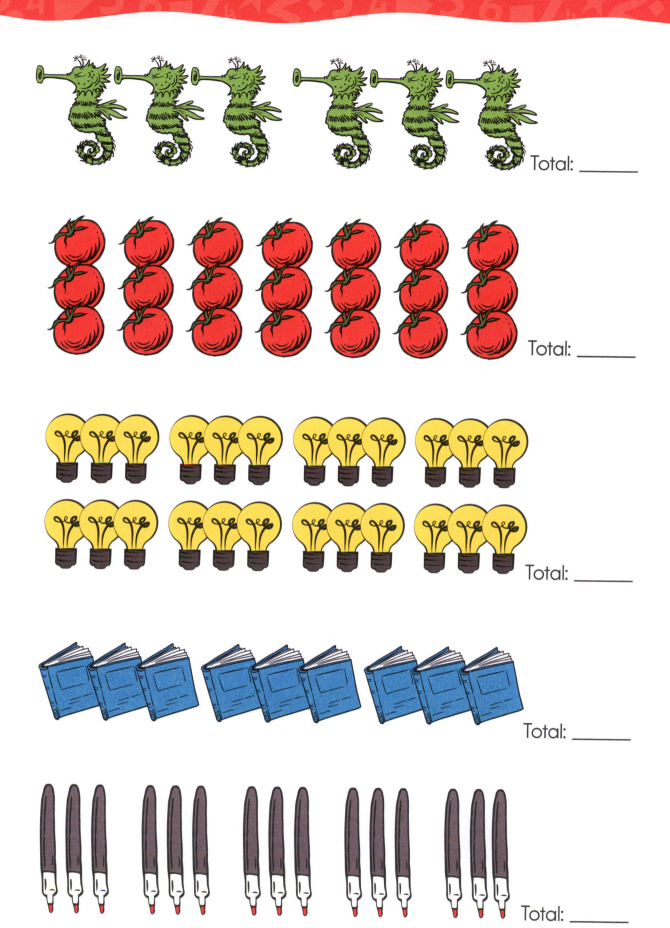

Total: _____

Total: _____

Total: _____

Total: _____

Total: _____

Skip Counting by Fours

Count by fours and write the number of apples on each tree.

_____ apples

_____ apples

_____ apples

Count by fours to get to the end of the maze.

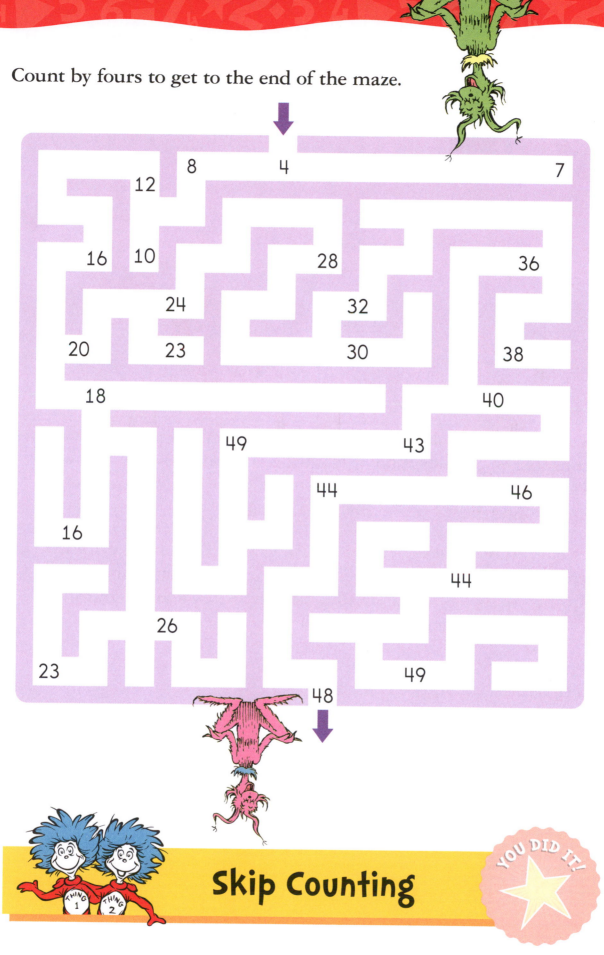

Skip Counting

YOU DID IT!

Exploring Values

When you learn about numbers,
then, sooner or later,
you should know which are **less than**
and which ones are **greater**.

We use the symbols **>** and **<** to compare numbers and show when a number is **greater than** or **less than** the number that follows. We can also use the equals sign (**=**) to show that the number is **equal to**, or the same as, the other number.

It's easy to remember which symbol to use. The larger number is always on the wide, open side of the symbol, while the smaller number is always at the small, closed point. When the numbers are equal, the open space is the same on both sides!

Write either **>** (greater than), **<** (less than), or **=** (equal to) so that each statement is correct.

12 ____ 4   6 ____ 88

33 ____ 53   71 ____ 34

Write the number of feet below each thing. Then write either > (greater than) or < (less than) in between them.

_____ _____ _____

_____ _____ _____

_____ _____ _____

Greater Than, Less Than

Write either > (greater than), < (less than), or = (equal to) so that each statement is correct. The first one has been done to show you how.

5 + 10   >   12

8 + 4   ___   21

3 + 9   ___   13

6 + 3   ___   9

11 + 4   ___   7

7 + 3   ___   12

Find a path to get the puppy to the yummy bone. When you get to each set of numbers, go in the direction of the greater number.

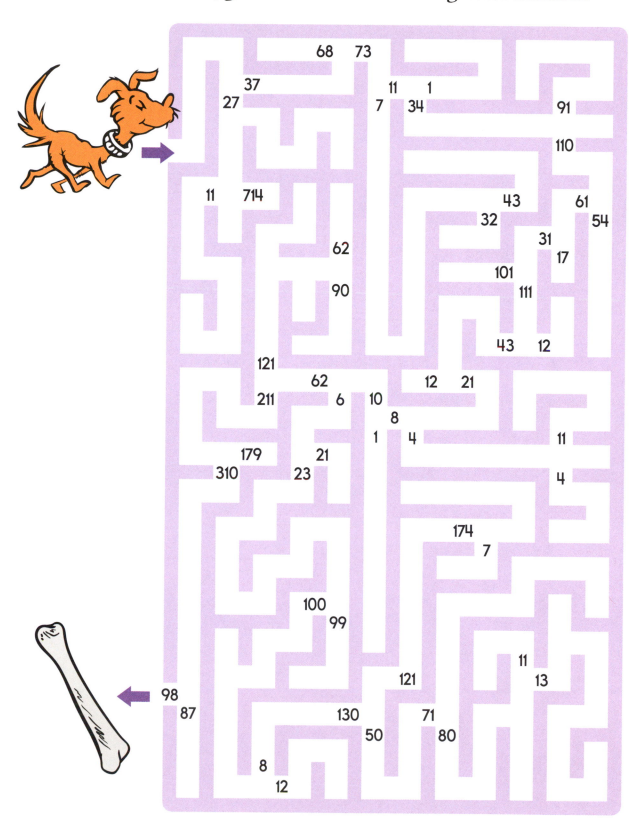

Graphs

Each of these musicians plays a different number of musical notes. The number of notes is shown on the graph. Circle the musician who plays the most notes. Draw a rectangle around the one who plays the fewest.

Circle the fox with the most socks. Draw rectangles around the foxes that have the same number of socks.

Making Graphs

A **graph** can help make sense of information.

152

For every two-footed character you see, make a **tally mark** (|). Do the same for characters that have four feet and characters that have six feet.

2	
4	
6	

Let's make a **bar graph**. Color one box for every tally mark you made.

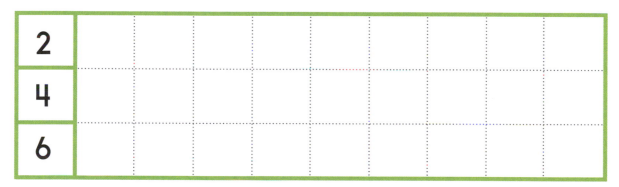

How many have two feet?_____

How many have four feet?_____

How many have six feet?_____

Estimation

Without counting, guess how many bricks are on this page.

Write that number. _____

Now count all the bricks and write the exact number. _____

Did you guess higher or lower? Did you get it just right?

Without counting, guess how many blocks are on this page.

Write that number. _____

Now count all the blocks and write the exact number. _____

Did you guess higher or lower? Did you get it just right?

Exploring Values

YOU DID IT!

Hooray for Letter E

Look at the words on this page and find the pairs of words that are the same, except one has an **E** at the end.

Now try it yourself.

Look around your home, and find three things that would become something else if you add a letter **E**.

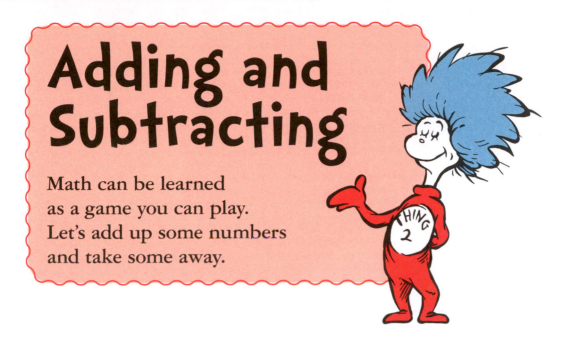

Adding and Subtracting

Math can be learned
as a game you can play.
Let's add up some numbers
and take some away.

Put a **+** or a **-** in each space to make each equation true.

5 _____ 2 = 7

9 _____ 1 = 10

24 _____ 3 = 21

99 _____ 1 = 98

$$4 \underline{\quad\quad} 4 = 8$$

$$15 \underline{\quad\quad} 5 = 10$$

$$8 \underline{\quad\quad} 8 = 0$$

Color in all the spaces that equal exactly five.

2 + 4	11 - 6	9 - 3	2 + 3
10 - 2	2 + 2	4 + 1	9 - 4
14 - 4	12 - 7	4 + 3	13 - 5
3 + 2	10 - 4	5 + 0	4 + 2
10 - 6	1 + 4	3 - 2	10 - 5
2 + 2	16 - 6	15 - 10	6 + 2

Add Single or Double Digits

Count and add the number of fruit. Then write the total.

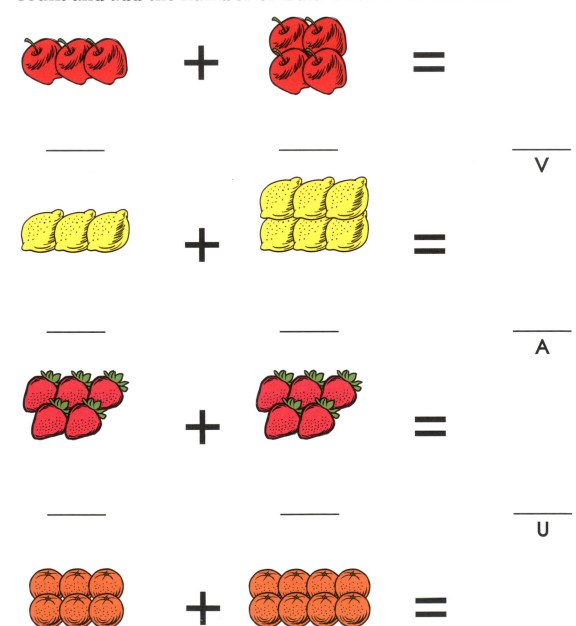

You Did It! Stickers

Place your stickers at the end of each lesson and on your certificates.

READING

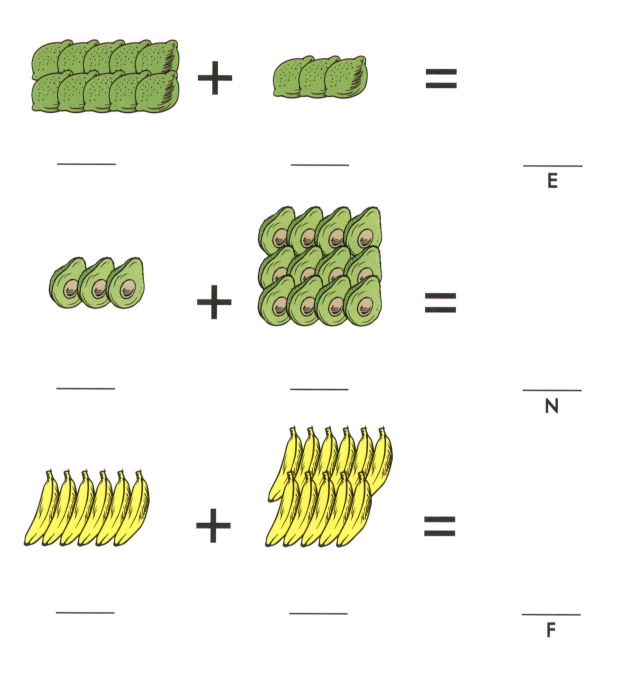

_____   +   _____   =   _____
                                                E

_____   +   _____   =   _____
                                                N

_____   +   _____   =   _____
                                                F

Reveal this message using the letter assigned to each answer.

_____   _____   _____   _____   _____   _____   _____
14   9   7   13   17   10   15

Subtract Single or Double Digits

Count and subtract the number of fruit. Then write the total.

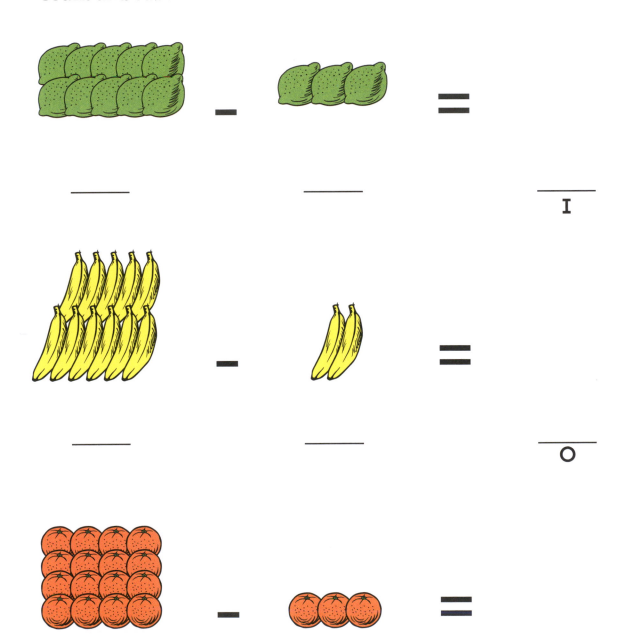

_____   _____   _____
                    I

_____   _____   _____
                    O

_____   _____   _____
                    Y

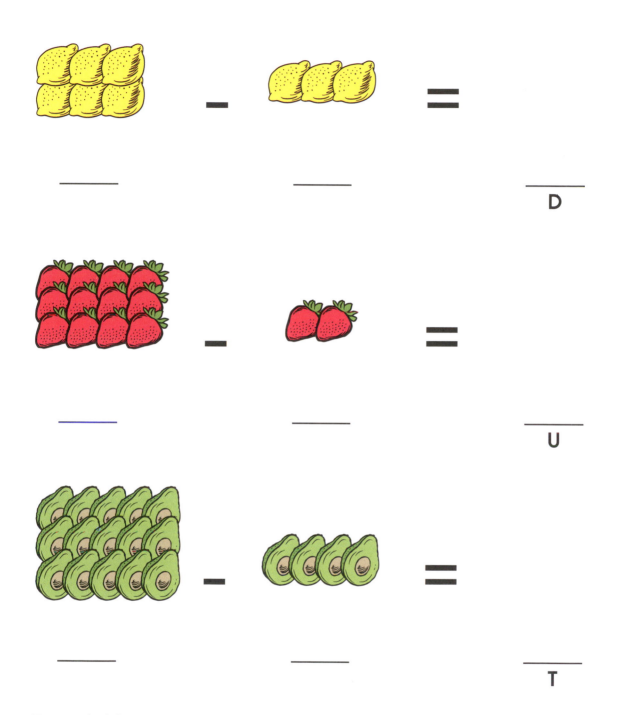

_____   _____   _____
                             D

_____   _____   _____
                             U

_____   _____   _____
                             T

Reveal this message using the letter assigned to each answer.

_____   _____   _____   _____   _____   _____   _____   _____
 13   9   10   3   7   3   7   11

Add or Subtract Single Digits

Find a path from top to bottom. You can only move through a number that is exactly two more than the number you are on.

Find a path from top to bottom. You can only move through a number that is exactly one less than the number you are on.

Adding and Subtracting

YOU DID IT!

Shapes, Measurement, Time, and Money

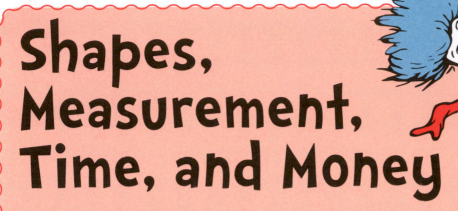

When you find a blue square or a circle that's pink,
it's a fine time to learn, measure, sort, count, or think.

Draw a line from each shape to its name.

triangle

hexagon

rectangle

square

circle

Find the hidden shapes in the picture and color them.

Color all the triangles blue. Color all the rectangles orange.
Color all the circles green.

Shapes and Colors

Find a path from top to bottom without crossing any red squares.

Find a path from top to bottom without crossing any orange circles.

More Shapes and Colors

Using the guide at the bottom of this page, write a letter in each shape.

Using the guide at the bottom of this page, write a letter in each shape.

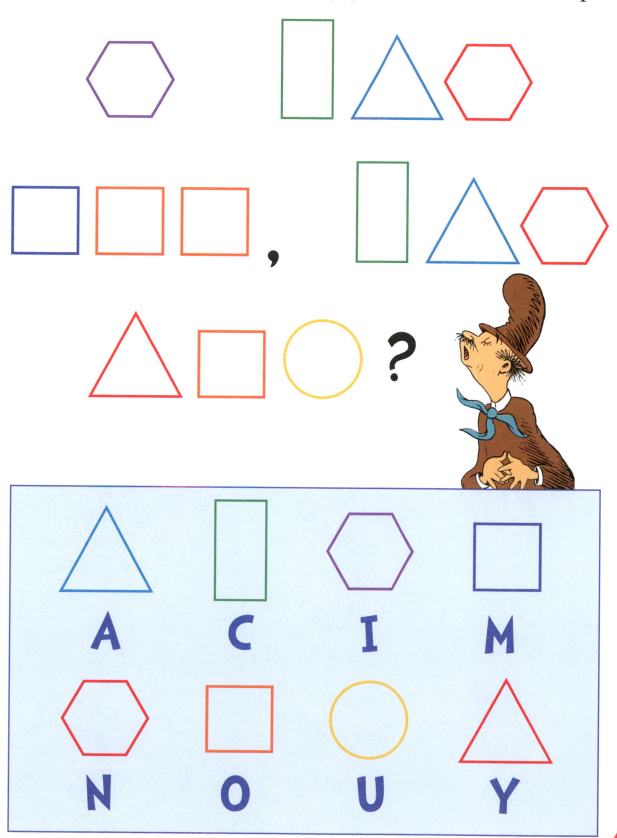

Dividing into Equal Parts

Draw a straight line so there are the same number of sunflowers on each side.

Draw a straight line so there are the same number of peppers on each side.

Draw two lines through this egg so there are four pieces with the same number of spots on each piece.

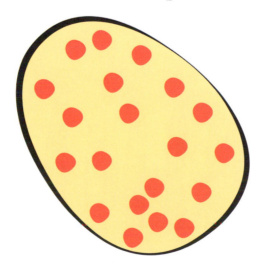

Patterns

What should go next? Color the missing item(s) in each group to complete the pattern.

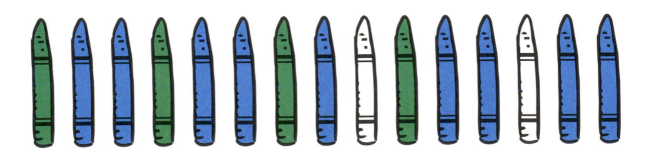

What should go next? Color the missing item(s) in each group to complete the pattern.

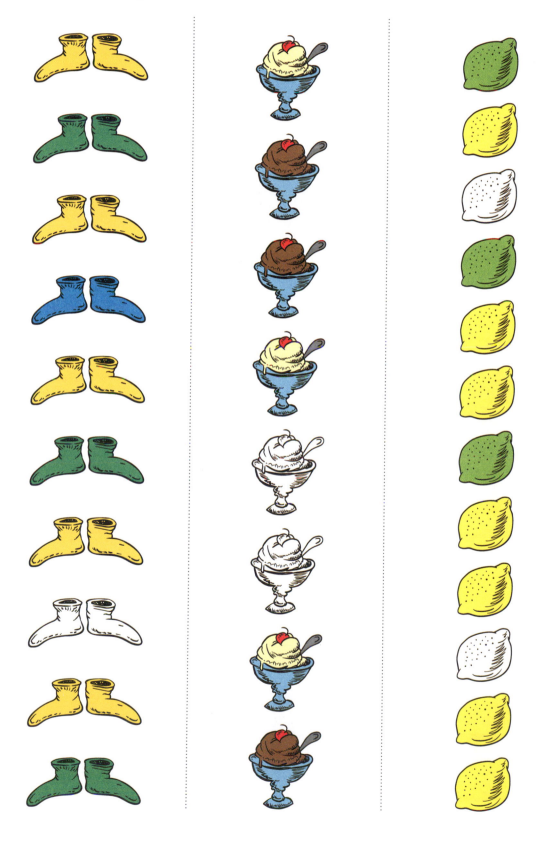

Measurement

Look at these objects and rulers. Circle the object that is the longest.

Circle the fish that is the longest.

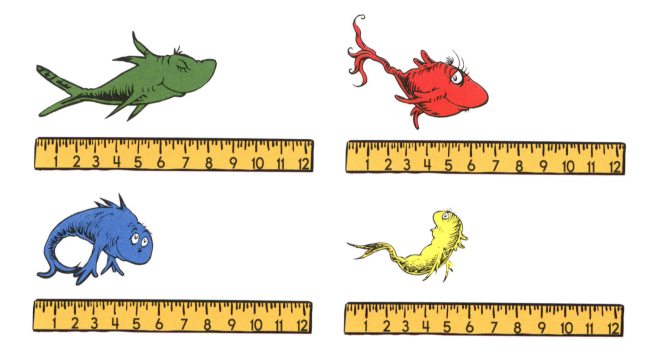

Circle the person who is the shortest.

Time

Draw lines to match each clock with the correct time.

4:35

9:30

2:50

12:15

Draw hands on each clock to show the time below it.

1:20

10:00

6:30

8:45

11:35

7:50

Money

Circle the group of coins that has a value of exactly fifty-five cents.

Penny	Nickel	Dime	Quarter
$0.01	$0.05	$0.10	$0.25

Circle the group of coins that has a value of exactly one dollar.

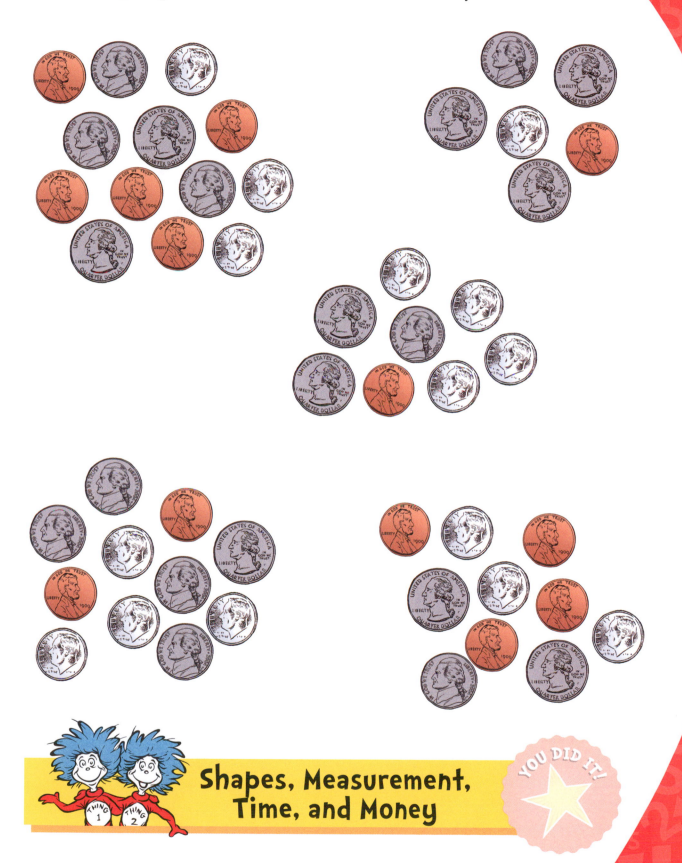

Certificate of Achievement

is presented to

_____

NAME

for becoming a

Math Magician!

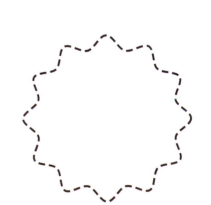

Today you are YOU, that is TRUER than true. There is NO ONE alive who is YOU-ER than YOU.

Collect your stickers at the end of each lesson.

Emotions

What makes you happy?
What makes you sad?
Let's talk about feelings,
Whether silly or glad!

Draw pictures of things that
make you feel happy or sad in
each box.

happy	sad

Circle three words that describe how you feel when you see this picture.

happy	silly
sad	afraid
mad	confident
nervous	surprised
confused	tired

Write two more words that describe how you feel when you see the picture.

_____   _____

In a Hurry? Don't Worry!

Circle the characters you think are in a hurry.
Draw a rectangle around the characters you think are sad.

Write a word to describe how Sam is feeling in each picture.
You can use the words in the box to help you.

| sad | happy | angry |
| surprised | proud | excited |

_____

_____

_____

_____

_____

_____

How Mad?

How do you look when you're just a little bit mad? Draw it.

How do you look when you're really, really mad? Draw it.

How do you feel at the end of the day? Draw yourself to show how you feel right before you go to bed.

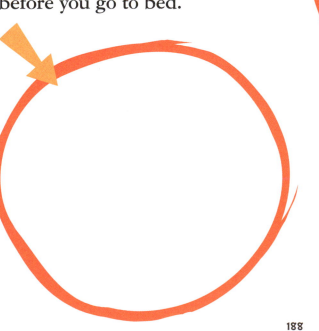

Put an X in the box next to the feeling that matches the picture.

☐ surprised   ☐ angry

☐ excited   ☐ sad

☐ surprised   ☐ angry

☐ excited   ☐ sad

☐ surprised   ☐ angry

☐ excited   ☐ sad

☐ surprised   ☐ angry

☐ excited   ☐ sad

Afraid, Content, Tired, Cheerful, Sad

Write a word that matches how each character is feeling.
Use the words in the word box to help you.

afraid	content	tired	cheerful	sad

_____ _____ _____

_____ _____

Draw a face on each person that matches the emotion.

tired

afraid

cheerful

sad

Identifying How Others Feel

Write how you think Bim and Ben feel in each picture.

Bim: _____

_____

Ben: _____

_____

Bim: _____

_____

Ben: _____

_____

Bim: _____

_____

Ben: _____

_____

What do you think this character might
say to you if you waved at it?

_____

_____

_____

_____

What do you think this character might
say to you if you met it?

_____

_____

_____

_____

Emotions

I See U

How many things can you find in this picture that have the letter U?

Now take the U challenge:
1. Find three things in your house that begin with a U.
2. Do three things that are spelled with words have a U in them.
3. Write the names of three people you know who have a U in their names.

Getting
Along

With your family and friends
is where you belong.
Let's share and learn
so we all get along.

Circle those that are getting along.
Draw a square around those that are
not getting along.

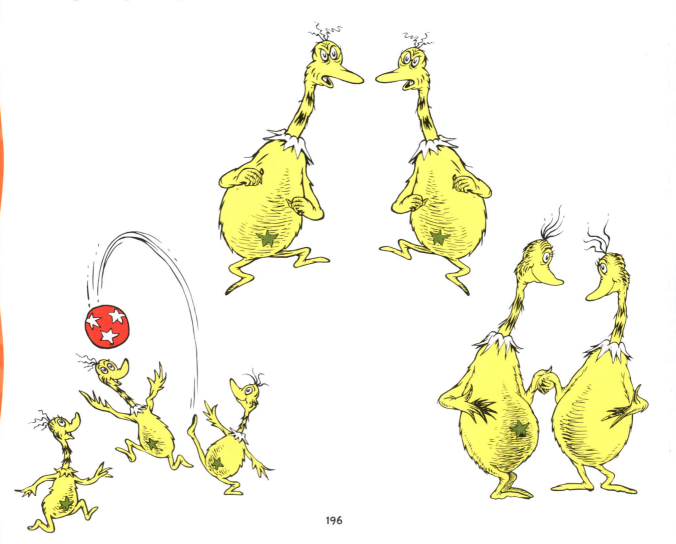

Draw a friend for each animal.

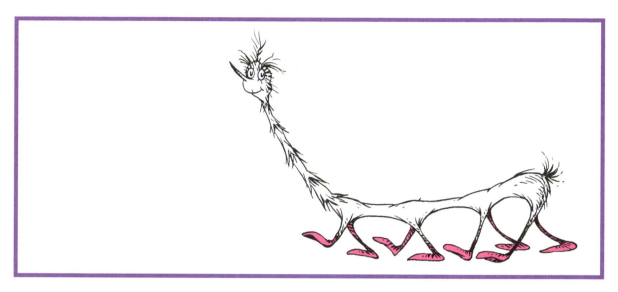

Wait!

Circle 👍 on the picture that shows someone being patient.

Circle 👎 on the picture that shows someone who didn't wait for their turn.

Write about a time when you had to be patient and wait to do something. Then draw a picture to show how you felt.

_____

_____

_____

_____

_____

_____

What Do They Want?

Draw lines to match things that would be fair trades.

Draw something that would make each character happy.

Following the Rules

Circle the situations in which everyone is following the rules.

Write one rule you have at home.

_____

_____

Write one rule you have at school.

_____

_____

Write one rule you have when you are in a car.

_____

_____

Getting Along

YOU DID IT!

They Were Odd

How many humps are on this wump? How many people are riding? Which of those numbers is even, and which is odd?

Now take the odd challenge:
Find something in your house that has exactly three of something. Then try to find something that comes in fives.

For a super challenge, look for something that comes in a group of seven.

Understanding Others

You'll have much more success
when you meet someone new
if you learn what things look like
from their point of view.

These four children saw an elephant at the zoo and had different reactions! Pick one character and write about what you think that person is feeling, and why you imagine they might be feeling that way.

Jasmine

Mateo

Aliah

Chad

_____

_____

_____

_____

_____

Write about the ways that you are the same as those pictured.

_____

_____

_____

_____

_____

_____

_____

_____

_____

The Things We All Need

Draw a line from the friend on the left
to the friend on the right who can help.

Circle one thing under each animal. Then write why they need it.

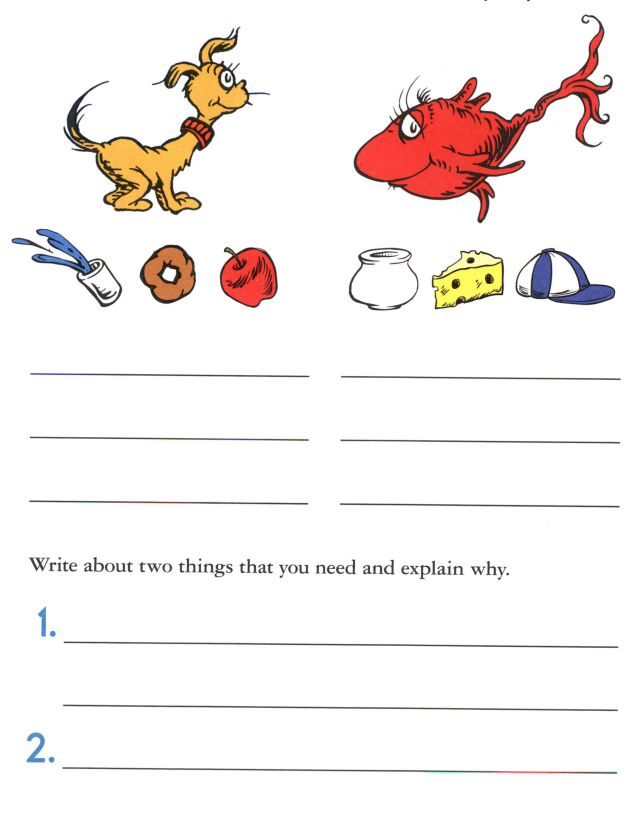

_____   _____

_____   _____

_____   _____

Write about two things that you need and explain why.

1. _____

_____

2. _____

_____

Friends

Write the name of a friend who would really like each of these things.

Draw a picture of yourself in this line, with a friend at each side.

Draw yourself and your friends doing your favorite outdoor activity.

Family

Write the name of someone in your family that each picture reminds you of.

_____

_____

_____

_____

Is there someone in your family who makes you laugh a lot? Write about them here.

_____

_____

_____

_____

Is there someone in your family who you like to spend quiet time with? Write about them here.

_____

_____

_____

_____

I'm the Only Me

What are four things you can do that many people can't do?

1. _____

2. _____

3. _____

4. _____

What are two things that make you special?

1. _____

_____

_____

2. _____

_____

_____

Draw something that most people don't like, but you do.

Draw something that everyone knows you like a lot.

Understanding Others

YOU DID IT!

Get Creative!

You can think and imagine,
and plan, and explain.
You can sure do a lot
With your wonderful brain!

Circle all the problems you see in this picture.

Write about how you can solve one of the problems you noticed.
Then draw a picture to show your solution.

_____

_____

_____

_____

_____

_____

_____

Real and Pretend

Circle things you could find in real life.
Draw a square around things that are imaginary.

Draw a picture of a new animal that lives here. Show them doing something that no one has done before.

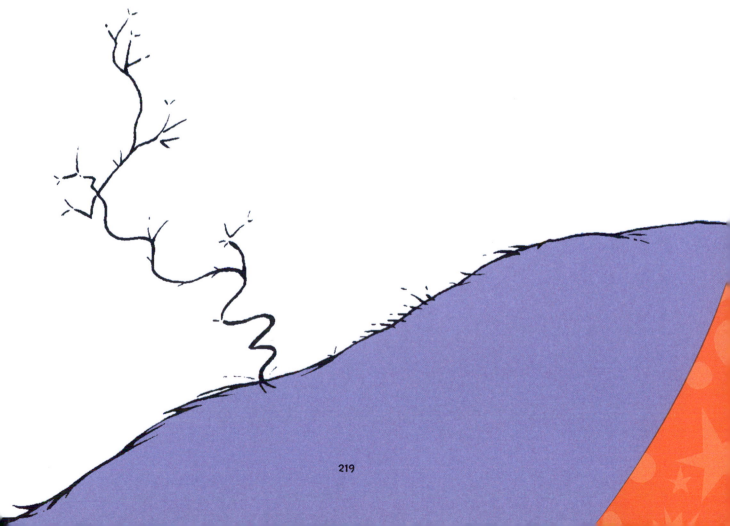

The Truth

Look at this scene. Circle **true** for the things that are true.
Circle **false** for the things that are not true.

The train is moving fast.   true   false

The trees are green.   true   false

Everybody is on the train.   true   false

The conductor is wearing a red hat.   true   false

The car is blue.   true   false

The car is on the ground.   true   false

Write something that is false about this picture.

_____

_____

Write something that is true about this picture.

_____

_____

Help Out

Draw everyone a pet.

Draw everyone some food.

Help this bear find a path home.

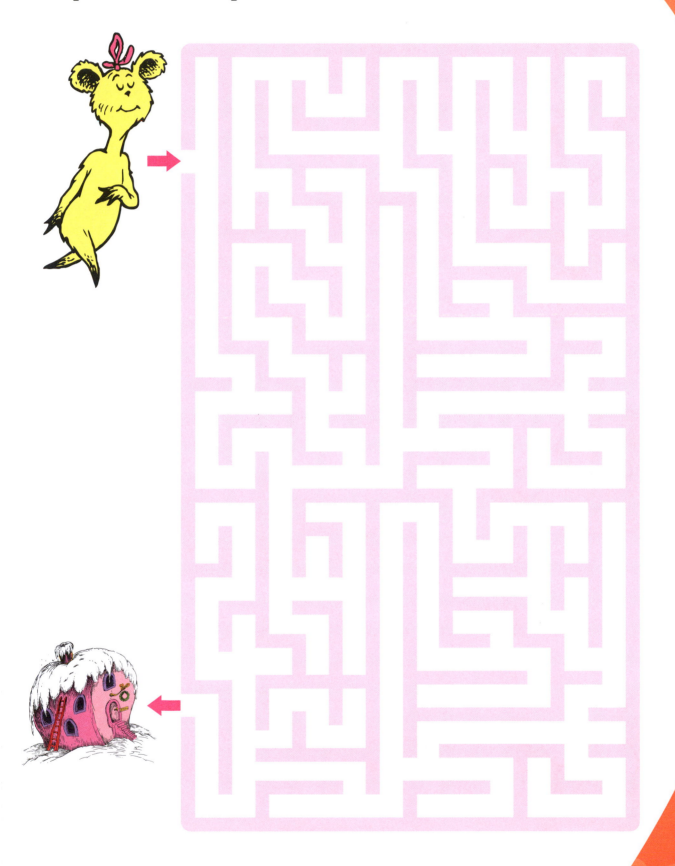

Tools and Rules

Write three things you can do with each of these objects.

1. _____
2. _____
3. _____

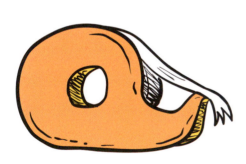

1. _____
2. _____
3. _____

1. _____
2. _____
3. _____

Write three rules that would make the place in the picture better.

1. _____

2. _____

3. _____

Write three things that would make the real world a better place.

1. _____

2. _____

3. _____

Invent It!

Draw and write about what this invention does.

_____

_____

_____

_____

_____

_____

Draw three things that are helping these pups fly.

Get Creative!

Communication

When you meet someone new
and you've both said hello,
keep talking, keep learning.
Oh, the things you can know!

Write a sentence about each
character. Who are they talking to?
What is being said?

_____

_____

_____

_____

_____

_____

_____

_____

_____

Unscramble the words to find ways people communicate.
Use the words in the word box to help you.

_____

t r e l e t

_____

m i l e a

_____

h o e n p l a l c

_____

x t t e

_____

c f e a o t c f e a

Making Sense

Look at the pictures, then write what you think could be happening in each one.

Write what the rabbit is hearing.

_____

_____

_____

Write what the bear is smelling.

_____

_____

_____

_____

_____

_____

Write what the worm is seeing.

_____

_____

_____

_____

_____

Face Your Fears

Oh no! This bear had a scary dream about losing his pants. Help him get through this maze of Snide bushes to find his pants and conquer his fear.

Write about a time when you faced a fear of yours.
Was it as scary as you expected?

_____

_____

_____

_____

_____

_____

_____

_____

Communication

Think and Drink

Look at this picture carefully. How many elephants are taking a drink of water?

Now think about how much water you drink. It's important to drink some water several times a day.

Keep a **water journal** for a week. Write down each time you drink some water and how much you drink.

Certificate of Achievement

is presented to

_____

NAME

for becoming a

Fantastic Friend!

SCIENCE

Think and **WONDER**. Wonder and **THINK**. How much **WATER** can fifty-five elephants **DRINK?**

Earth Science

Earth is one of eight planets that travel laps around the sun. It takes 365 days for Earth to complete just one.

Mercury is closest to the sun.
Next comes Venus.
Earth is the third planet.
Mars is the red planet. It comes after Earth.
Jupiter is the biggest planet.
It is the fifth planet from the sun.
Saturn has rings made of acid.
It comes after Jupiter.
Uranus and Neptune are the two farthest planets.

Label each planet.

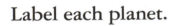

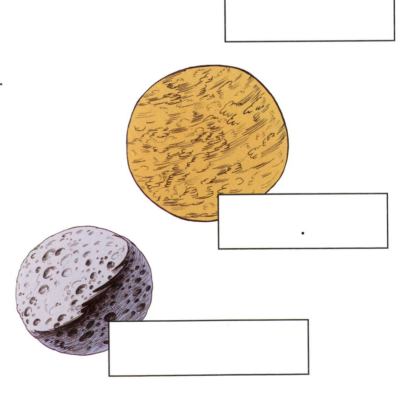

What planet do we live on?

_____

Our Solar System

Complete each sentence. Use the words in the word box to help you.

star	solar system	constellation
planet	moon	sun

Earth is a _____.

Earth travels around the _____.

The sun and all its planets make up the _____ _____.

The sun is a _____.

The _____ travels around Earth.

A pattern of stars is called a _____.

The moon circles Earth. Sometimes we see the moon during the day. Sometimes we see it at night. Sometimes we do not see it at all.

We say the moon goes through **phases**. From big and round like a ball, to half a circle, to a thin sliver, like a fingernail.

Read and copy the name of each phase of the moon.

new
moon _____

waning
crescent _____

first
quarter _____

full
moon _____

last
quarter _____

waxing
crescent _____

Seasons of the Year

Match the season to its picture.

winter

spring

summer

autumn

What is another word for autumn?

_____

A **thermometer** (pronounced **ther-mom-i-ter**) tells you how hot or cold it is. 0°F is a cold temperature. 100°F is hot.

Read each thermometer. Write the temperature, then circle whether it is hot or cold.

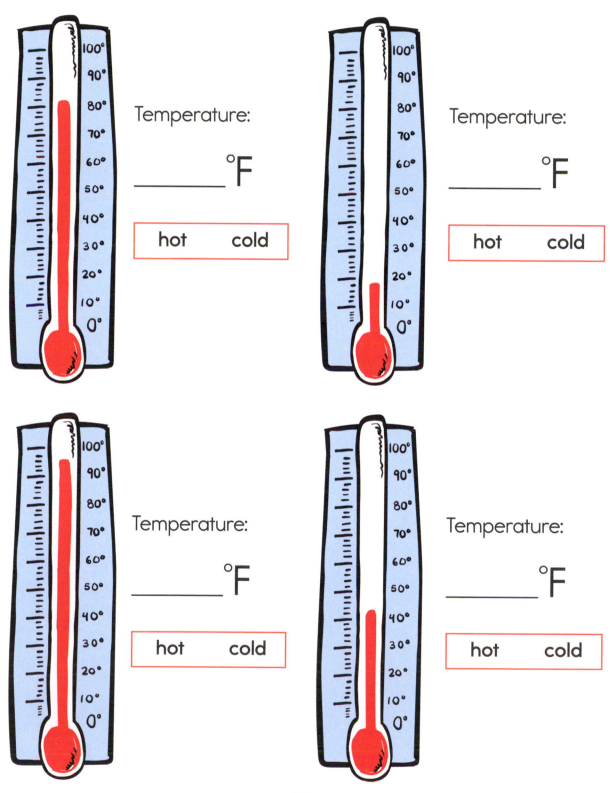

Temperature:

_____°F

| hot | cold |

Temperature:

_____°F

| hot | cold |

Temperature:

_____°F

| hot | cold |

Temperature:

_____°F

| hot | cold |

Weather

Match the weather word to its picture.

snow

wind

rain

sun

clouds

What is the weather like today?

_____

Is it cold or hot?

_____

Is it day or night?

_____

Is it cloudy or clear?

_____

What is your favorite kind of weather?

_____

Draw a picture that shows your favorite kind of weather.

Environments

When it's cold outside your home, it could be very hot somewhere else. The weather is different in different places all over the world.

Write two types of weather for each environment.

| hot | wet | snowy |
| cold | dry | rainy |

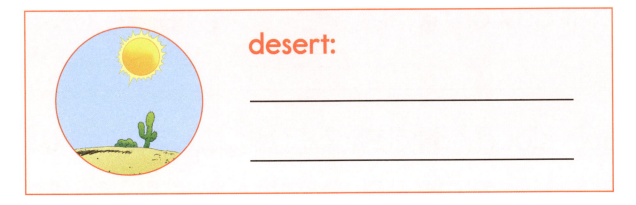

desert:

_____

_____

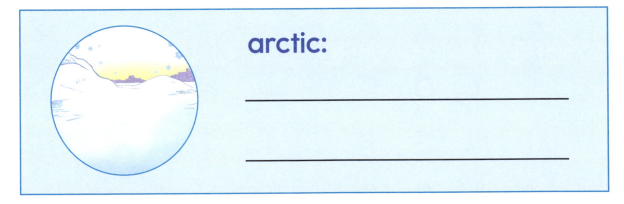

arctic:

_____

_____

rainforest:

_____

_____

Find and circle the weather words hidden among the letters. Look for them up, down, across, and diagonally. Use the words in the word box to help you.

thunder	rain	sun
lightning	hail	storm
tornado	sleet	earthquake

R A H B U Q O R S J E

E H F P H D R L L E K

D Z A R A D A I E V A

N C A N P O N G E A U

U W R W R N U H T S Q

H O A A C E S T C G H

T L I D R X O N L Z T

U I N F F P D I R C R

Y Q Q V R A A N E W A

S T O R M H Y G D Y E

Earth Science

247

In the Dark

Look at the mysterious shapes on this page. What do you think they really are? Try to guess the ordinary things that make up the shapes.

Now play a shadow game! Use your hands or items you find in your home. Try to make shadows that look like animals or other things.

Life Science

All living things grow and change.
They feel the world—it's true.
A tree, a fly, and you and I
are all living things, too!

Circle the items that all living things need.

Put a **P** next to each **plant**. Put an **A** next to each **animal**. Put an **X** next to the **nonliving things**.

Plants

Label the parts of a plant.

roots	stem	leaf	flower

Draw a seed.	Draw a plant.	Draw a tomato.

A **fruit** grows on a tree or vine. It has seeds inside.
A **vegetable** grows in the ground. You eat its stem, leaves, or roots.

Put an X in the box next to the correct description for each picture.

☐ fruit   ☐ vegetable

☐ fruit   ☐ vegetable

☐ fruit   ☐ vegetable

☐ fruit   ☐ vegetable

☐ fruit   ☐ vegetable

☐ fruit   ☐ vegetable

Animals and Their Habitats

Read the directions in each box. Label each animal part you circle.
Use the words in the word box to help you.

foot	wing	fur	fin

Circle one part of the fish that helps it live in water.

_____

Circle one part of the mountain goat that helps it live in the mountains.

_____

Circle the part of the polar bear that helps it live in the snow.

_____

Circle the part of the bird that helps it fly.

_____

Where does it live? Draw a line to match each animal to its home.

Parents and Babies

Match the animal parent to its baby.

How do animal parents help their babies?
Connect the words to the pictures.

food

shelter

protection

What is another way animal parents help their babies?

_____

Animals That Lay Eggs

Number the stages of the life cycle of a butterfly.

1

6

Who lays eggs?

Circle the animals that lay eggs.
When the egg hatches, a baby animal is born!

Life Science

YOU DID IT!

Health

Food and water, sleep and rest,
hard work and time to play.
These all help us stay healthy.
We need them every day.

You have five senses that give you information about the world around you. Write the correct word to finish each sentence.

| ears | mouth | eyes | nose | hands |

I touch things with my _____.

I smell things with my _____.

I see things with my _____.

I taste things with my _____.

I hear things with my _____.

Connect the eye to the words for **sight**.
Connect the hand to the words for **touch**.
Connect the mouth to the words for **taste**.

pretty

sweet

soft

dark

itchy

sour

261

Caring for Your Body

Circle the foods that are good for your teeth.

Write what each thing is used for.

_____   _____

_____   _____

_____   _____

_____   _____

_____   _____

_____   _____

Healthy Foods

Eat healthy food to keep your body fueled up and ready to go!

Circle the foods you can eat that are good for you.
Put an X over the things that you cannot eat or drink.

whole-grain bread

fruit

oven mitt

vegetables

lightbulb

water

Write some of your favorite foods.

_____   _____

_____   _____

Fill this plate with healthy foods. Be sure to include plenty of fruits and vegetables with your meal.

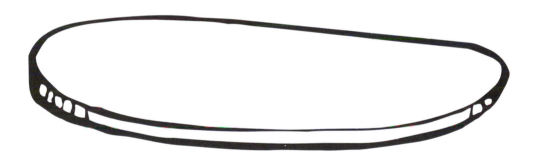

An afternoon snack gives you energy to keep going. Draw your favorite snack.

Exercise

There are so many ways you can move your body and have fun.

Circle the things you can do that are good for you.
Put an X over images that do not show something healthy.

Write and draw an activity you like to do that is good for you.

_____

_____

_____

_____

_____

Staying Safe

Circle the ones who are being safe.

Traffic signals tell you when it's safe to go.

Red means stop.
Green means go.
Yellow means slow.

Follow the traffic signals through the maze,
avoiding any red traffic signals.

Health

Physical Science

Light and sound are all around.
They reach out from far away.
Sound waves help you hear things.
Light waves light the way.

Some things give off light. Some things make sounds. Some do both.

A **Venn diagram** tells you how things are alike and how they're different. Each thing you compare has its own outer circle. The area where they come together shows the things they have in common.

Place these objects where they belong in the Venn diagram.

television	flashlight	fireplace	radio
dog	candle	lighthouse	cell phone

light   both   sound

Circle the sounds you have heard. Draw a star on each sound that you think is loud.

airplane	whisper	duck quacking	fire truck siren	screaming
car horn	train	vacuum	mouse	drums
television	dog barking	raindrops	ocean waves	bird chirping
bear growling	faucet	cat purring	baby crying	balloons popping
fireworks	snoring	bee buzzing	radio	bells

Which sound do you think is the loudest?

_____

Which sound do you think is the softest?

_____

Light

Light comes from different places, like a lamp or the sun. When light shines on something, it becomes lighter. When something is in the way, it makes a shadow.

The tree is in between the sun and the ground. Look at the tree's shadow on the ground.

Draw the object's shadow.

Match the pictures to their shadows.

Sound

Things that are close sound louder than things that are far away. Circle the person who sounds louder.

If you yell, will your voice get louder or softer?

_____

When you whisper, does your voice sound louder or softer?

_____

Loud or soft?
Sort these sounds into the correct box.

| cat purring | band | bird chirping | concert |
| fire truck | whistle | whisper | baby crying |

loud

_____

_____

_____

_____

_____

soft

_____

_____

_____

_____

_____

Properties

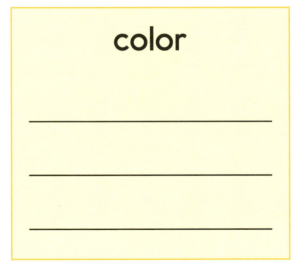

Matter is anything that has weight and takes up space.

We use scientific words to describe how things look and feel.

Sort the words into the box that tells what they describe.

circle	green
blue	thin
soft	square
big	bumpy
triangle	red
small	hard

size

_____

_____

_____

color

_____

_____

_____

shape

_____

_____

_____

texture

_____

_____

_____

Compare these two things. How are they alike? How are they different? Use words that describe their **size, color, shape,** and **texture.**

Matter

Matter can be **solid**, **liquid**, or **gas**.

Complete the sentences with one of the three types of matter.

Water takes the shape of whatever you put it in. It is a _____.

When water is frozen, it turns to ice. Ice is a _____.

When water is very hot, it turns to steam. Steam is a _____.

Snow is a _____.

Rain is a _____.

Label the pictures **solid**, **liquid**, or **gas**.

_____   _____

_____   _____

_____   _____

Physical Science

Engineering Design

An invention starts with a question.
It starts with a why or a how.
If a question's in need of an answer,
you can try to solve it right now!

If you like to find problems and solve them,
you could be a great engineer.
You must test and invent and try, try again
until the solution is clear.

What is **engineering**? An **engineer** thinks about problems and finds solutions.

Read and copy these engineering words.

observe _____

ask _____

invent _____

discover _____

explore _____

Inventions make life easier. Match the machine to the task.

looking
at stars

avoiding
traffic jams

looking at
small objects

seeing in
the dark

traveling long
distances

Scientific Process

Complete each sentence. Use the words in the word box to help you.

test ask	share write	imagine create	scientific process

When you do an experiment to explore a new idea, follow the steps in the

_____ _____:

_____ a question,

_____ what will happen,

make a plan to _____ your guess,

_____ your experiment,

_____ down what happens,

and _____ what you learned.

A boat and a fork are both made of matter. The boat is heavy, but the boat can float. The fork is light, but it cannot float.

Some things push away the water. That makes them float. If something does not push away the water, it will sink.

Complete each sentence. Use the words in the word box to help you.

sink	float	light	push	matter	pull

Everything you can touch is made of _____.

When you use force to move a thing closer to you: _____

The opposite of pull: _____

Go to the bottom: _____

Stay on top: _____

The opposite of heavy: _____

Science Tools

Match the name to the science tool.

telescope

scale

measuring cup

pencil

calculator

magnet

284

Find and circle the science terms hidden among the letters. Look for them up, down, across, and diagonally. Use the words in the word box to help you.

float	matter	question	sound	energy
sink	experiment	process	light	invention

H M L D A T R S Q I E

E B H C E I J P L N Q

T D I E N T T F U V R

N E G S E I T S B E L

E I H N R H E D I N P

M O A O G Y N L C T R

I A D I Y U F A W I O

R N L T O V L R A O C

E U A S S E O S T N E

P A K E A P A O I D S

X H T U L R T E R N S

E N U Q M A T T E R K

Machines

What's missing? Draw in the missing parts of the car.

What does the steering wheel do?

_____

What does the engine do?

_____

What is a seatbelt for?

_____

Label the parts of the computer.

mouse	keyboard	screen

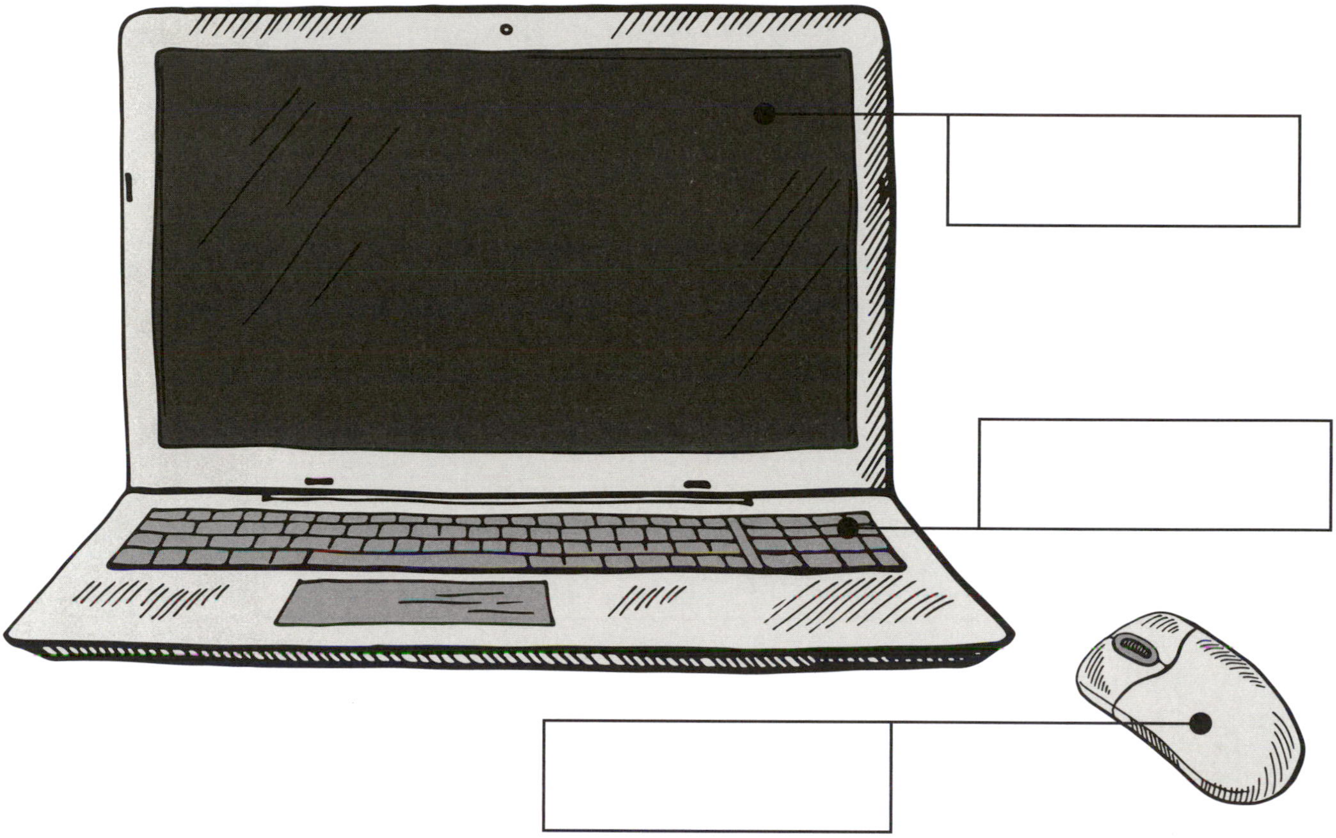

Circle the things you can use a computer for.

nap   write

draw   eat

read   run

Inventions

Inventors create things that can help us do things faster or better or easier.

Long ago, books were written on paper by hand. It took a long time just to make one book. After the **printing press** was invented, many books could be printed in just a little bit of time.

Today, people still read books on paper, but they can also read them on **laptops** and **phone screens** without using any paper at all.

Use words from the word box to make the story true.

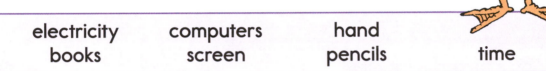

| electricity | computers | hand | |
| books | screen | pencils | time |

Books used to be written by _____.

The printing press made it easier to

create many _____ in very little time.

Today, you can read from a book or a

computer _____. It takes a lot less

_____ to make a book these days!

If you were an inventor and could create a machine that helps make your everyday life easier, what would it do?

_____

_____

_____

What would you call it?

_____

Draw a picture of it.

Engineering Design

EXPLORE **YOUR** WORLD!

Match Up

Look at this picture carefully. Can you spot the one character whose gloves are the same color?

Now go on a matching mission. Look for all the gloves in your home. Try to see if each one has a match.

That was just the warm-up. Now try it... with socks!

Certificate of Achievement

is presented to

NAME

for becoming a

Science Superstar!

Answers

Page 8
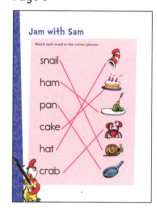

Jam with Sam

Match each word to the correct picture.

snail
ham
pan
cake
hat
crab

Page 9

Circle all the words that have the letter A in them.

pine	(bat)
(pan)	(sat)
rug	bin
(rake)	sun
(happy)	(stare)
bite	fine
(rate)	fun
rot	jog

Page 10
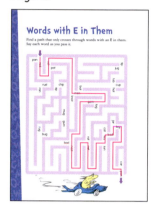

Words with E in Them

Find a path that only crosses through words with an E in them. Say each word as you pass it.

Page 11
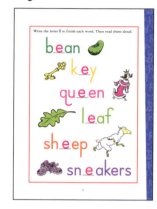

Write the letter E to finish each word. Then read them aloud.

b_ea_n
k_e_y
qu_ee_n
l_ea_f
sh_ee_p
sn_e_akers

Page 12

Words with I in Them

Circle all the words that are spelled with an I in them.

rug	(jig)
(pig)	(slide)
(hit)	(ride)
hot	(fish)
(kind)	(big)
log	(dig)
(wig)	pot

Page 13
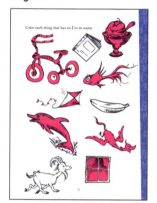

Color each thing that has an I in its name.

Page 14
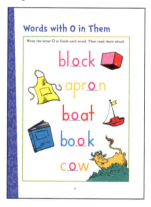

Words with O in Them

Write the letter O to finish each word. Then read them aloud.

bl_o_ck
apr_o_n
b_o_at
b_oo_k
c_o_w

Page 15
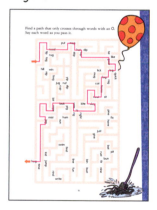

Find a path that only crosses through words with an O. Say each word as you pass it.

Page 16
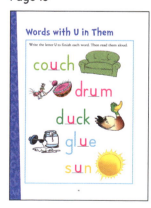

Words with U in Them

Write the letter U to finish each word. Then read them aloud.

co_u_ch
dr_u_m
d_u_ck
gl_u_e
s_u_n

Page 17

Circle all the words that are spelled with a U in them.

hog	(fun)
(cut)	win
zip	tar
(bun)	(hug)
(run)	fig
(hut)	dog
pin	(cub)
rat	sip

Page 18

Chippity Chop

Circle nine things that end in -ip.
Draw a square around nine things that end in -op.

(chip)	(hip)
sap	[flop]
[chop]	(clip)
(flip)	wrap
	[slop]
	nap

Page 19

hop	(dip)
clop	tip
map	rip
whip	(drip)
pop	shop
bop	plop

Get Ready, Readers!

293

Page 20

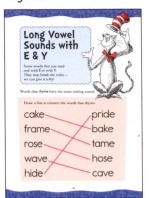

Long Vowel Sounds with E & Y

Some words that you read end with E or with Y. They may break the rules— we can give it a try!

Words that rhyme have the same ending sound.

Draw a line to connect the words that rhyme.

cake — pride
frame — bake
rose — tame
wave — hose
hide — cave

Page 21

Find and circle the words that end in E or Y hidden among the letters. Look for them up, down, across, or diagonally. Use the words in the word box to help you.

candy — cane — rate — sky
try — sunny — July — bunny
cute — ripe — baby

H A U K G Q K S E J L
R N Y Z X Y B K G Q R
C A H S U N N Y F D B
V I T A R E V O V F I
M A N E S T G B A B Y
P T N F Q U V W O Q G
W E C U W C J U L Y B
Y N A U R I A T G J Q
Q Y N H V I X N O R N
T B E W S P P W D D N
B R E N Z B Y E B Y F
G I Y N P L V K T I F

Page 22

The Amazing Letter E

Copy the word from the left to each space on the right. You'll make a new word each time!

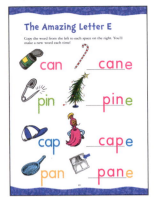

can — cane
pin — pine
cap — cape
pan — pane

Page 23

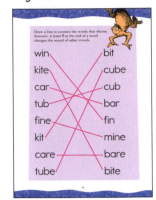

Draw a line to connect the words that rhyme. Remember: A letter E at the end of a word changes the sound of other vowels.

win — bit
kite — cube
car — cub
tub — bar
fine — fin
kit — mine
care — bare
tube — bite

Page 24

Hooray for the Letter E!

Unscramble each set of letters to spell words that end in E. Use the words in the word box to help you.

fire — care — bone — fuse

care
r c a e

bone
e o b n

fire
r e f i

fuse
s f e u

Page 25

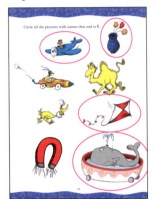

Circle all the pictures with names that end in E.

Page 26

Ending in Y

Circle all the pictures with names that end in Y.

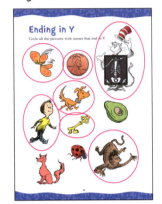

Page 27

Find a path that only crosses through words ending in Y.

Page 35

Write the words that had one syllable in the green box. Write the words that had two syllables in the orange box.

one syllable	two syllables
come	about
first	many
from	water
word	mother
one	follow
said	number
the	other
these	people

Page 40

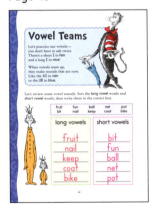

Vowel Teams

Let's practice our vowels— you don't have to ask twice. There's a short I in him and a long I in nice!

When vowels team up, they make sounds that are new. Like the AI in rain or the UE in blue.

Let's review some vowel sounds. Sort the long vowel words and short vowel words, then write them in the correct box.

fruit — fun — ball — net — pot
bit — nail — keep — coat — bike

long vowels	short vowels
fruit	bit
nail	fun
keep	ball
coat	net
bike	pot

Page 41

Color the pictures with names that have long vowel sounds blue. Color the pictures with names that have short vowel sounds red.

Page 42

Long A Pairs

Circle the words that have a long A made by AI. Draw a rectangle around the words where AY makes the long A sound.

rain	say
day	tray
play	wait
stay	tail
pain	pay
main	clay
mail	bait

Page 43

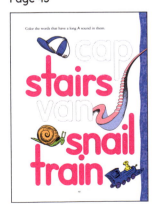

Color the words that have a long A sound in them.

cap stairs van snail train

Page 44

Long E Pairs

Circle the words that have a long E sound made by EE. Put a box around the words where EY makes the long E sound.

chimney	deer
hockey	feet
key	freeze
meet	green
donkey	knee
queen	need
free	valley

Page 45

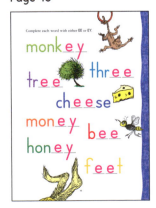

Complete each word with either EE or EY.

monkey
tree
three
cheese
money
bee
honey
feet

Page 46

Long O Pairs

Circle the words that have a long O made by OA. Put a box around the words where OE makes the O sound.

boat	road
coat	soap
toe	goal
coal	foe
hoe	soak
goat	loan
doe	woe

Page 47

Write the long O words next to each picture.

boat

soap

goat

coat

Page 48

AU and AW

Read each word aloud.
Copy the words with AU into the AU box.
Copy the words with AW into the AW box.

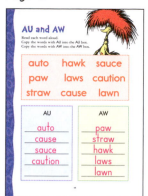

auto	hawk	sauce
paw	laws	caution
straw	cause	lawn

AU	AW
auto	paw
cause	straw
sauce	hawk
caution	laws
	lawn

Page 49

Color the words with AU blue.
Color the words with AW green.

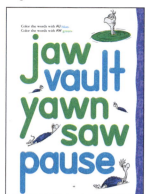

jaw
vault
yawn
saw
pause

Page 50

E Vowel Combinations

IE makes a long I sound. Write IE to complete each word.

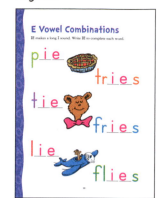

pie

tries

tie

fries

lie

flies

Page 51

UE makes a long U sound. Write UE to complete each word.

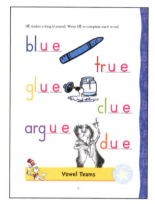

blue

true

glue

clue

argue

due

Vowel Teams

Page 52

Hardworking Letters

Some powered-up letters make more than one sound. The letters O, C, and G are the hardest workers around!

Read each word aloud.
Sort them by the sound OO makes.

| look | cook | hook | room | too |
| took | good | roof | moo | pool |

OO as in "moon"	OO as in "book"
roof	look
room	took
moo	cook
too	good
pool	hook

Page 55

OW can also make a long O sound. Let's compare the two OW sounds.
Read each word aloud. Sort them by the sound OW makes.

glow	clown	snow
towel	brown	grow
power	shower	flow

OW as in "bow"	OW as in "owl"
glow	towel
snow	power
grow	clown
flow	brown
	shower

Page 56

Hard and Soft C

When C comes before A, O, or U, it makes a K sound. This is a hard C.
When C comes before E, I, or Y, it makes an S sound. This is a soft C.

Say the name of each picture. Circle the ones that make an S sound. Draw a rectangle around the ones that make a K sound. Hint: The sound you are looking for might not be at the start of the word.

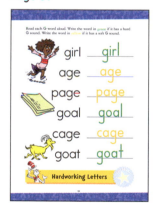

Write the word that has both a hard and a soft C.

circle

Page 57

Read each word aloud. If the C makes a K sound, color it blue.
If the C makes an S sound, color it red.

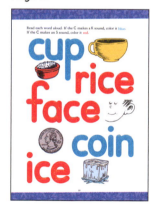

cup
rice
face
coin
ice

Page 58

Hard and Soft G

The letter G makes two sounds, too. It can sound hard, as in grape, or it can sound soft, as in germ.

Say the name of each picture. Circle the pictures with names that make a hard G sound. Draw a rectangle around the ones that make a soft G sound.

Write the word that has both a hard and a soft G.

garbage can

Page 59

Read each G word aloud. Write the word in green if it has a hard G sound. Write the word in blue if it has a soft G sound.

girl — girl

age — age

page — page

goal — goal

cage — cage

goat — goat

Hardworking Letters

Page 60

Consonant Blends

When consonants combine to make sounds, those letters form a blend. They can show up anyplace in a word—the beginning, middle, or end.

Put an X in the box next to the blend that is found in each word.

| ☐ bl ☒ sl | ☒ bl ☐ sl |
| ☐ fl ☐ cl | ☐ fl ☐ cl |

| ☐ bl ☐ sl | ☐ bl ☐ sl |
| ☒ fl ☐ cl | ☒ fl ☐ cl |

Page 61

Write the correct blend to complete each word.

blue

glue

clam

Read and copy these words with consonant blends.

play _____

flap _____

clay _____

slip _____

Page 62

R Blends

These words are missing their beginning letters. Write in the R blend to complete each word. Use the letters in the box to help you.

| cr | fr | pr | tr | gr |

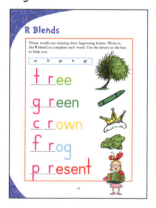

tree

green

crown

frog

present

Page 63

Circle the R blend that appears in the name of each object.

tr / dr

gr / tr

gr / br

dr / fr

br / cr

gr / br

Page 64

S Blends

These words are missing their beginning letters. Write in the S blend to complete each word. Use the letters in the box to help you.

| sl | sp | st | sw | sm |

stop

spoon

slug

sweet

smile

295

Page 65

Some S blends have three letters.
Put an X in the box next to the blend that is found in each word.

☐ sl ☐ scr
☐ squ ☒ str

☐ spl ☐ scr
☐ sm ☐ str

☐ spl ☒ scr
☐ squ ☐ sw

☐ spl ☐ scr
☒ squ ☐ sp

Page 66

T Blends

Add TH to complete each word.

th**ink**
th**at**   th**is**
too th
mo th   ma th
ba th

Page 67

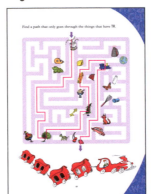

Find a path that only goes through the things that have TR.

Page 68

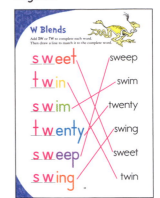

W Blends

Add SW or TW to complete each word.
Then draw a line to match it to the complete word.

sweet — sweep
twin — swim
swim — twenty
twenty — swing
sweep — sweet
swing — twin

Page 69

Circle the words that begin with a consonant blend.

flip   three   plate
clip   tree   free
cat   tap   drum
blue   cake   saw

Write the words you circled.

flip   tree
clip   plate
blue   free
three   drum

Page 70

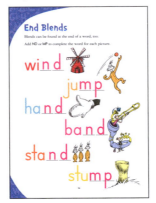

End Blends

Blends can be found at the end of a word, too.
Add ND or MP to complete the word for each picture.

wi**nd**
ju**mp**
ha**nd**
ba**nd**
sta**nd**
stu**mp**

Page 71

Complete the words. Use clues from the sentences to figure out
which word is correct. Use the letters in the box to help you.

rd   rt   rm   rn   rp

I can't wait for
school to sta**rt**.

The tree blew over in the sto**rm**.

It was not very ha**rd**
to find you over there.

You play that song on
the ha**rp** very well.

The animals are safe in the ba**rn**.

Page 72

End Blends with L and N

Put an X in the box next to the blend that is found at the end of
the name for each picture.

☒ nk ☐ lt
☒ lt ☐ lk
☒ lk ☐ st
☐ st ☒ nk

Page 73

Circle the words that end with a consonant blend.

act   melt   best
fact   bed   pool
face   link   cart
card   most   feel

Write the words you circled.

act   link
fact   most
card   best
melt   cart

Consonant Blends

Page 74

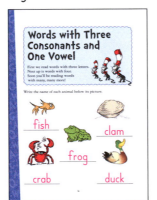

Words with Three Consonants and One Vowel

First we read words with three letters.
Next up is words with four.
Soon you'll be reading words
with many, many more!

Write the name of each animal below its picture.

fish   clam
frog
crab   duck

Page 75

Mix and Match the word beginnings and
endings to make new words. Put the words
that make sense in the **real** column. Put the
nonsense words in the **silly** column.

beginnings	TH	CH	SH
endings	IN	IP	OP	UT

real	silly
thin	thip
chin	thop
chip	thut
chop	chut
shin	
ship	
shop	
shut	

Page 76

CVCC Words

These pages have words that begin with
a consonant, then a vowel, followed by two more consonants.
Circle the word that matches the picture.

set   (nest)   (lamp)   lime
net   nets   camp   tame

tart   tens   belt   (bell)
teen   (tent)   bent   labs

Page 78

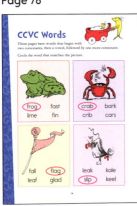

CCVC Words

These pages have words that begin with
two consonants, then a vowel, followed by one more consonant.
Circle the word that matches the picture.

(frog)   fast   (crab)   bark
lime   fin   crib   cars

fall   (flag)   leak   kale
leaf   glad   (slip)   keel

Page 80

Powerful Pairs

Circle the CCVC or CVCC word that matches the picture.

slip   (clam)
(swim)   climb
seal   crib

vine   (ship)
(vest)   shop
vast   flip

pack   fire
(plum)   four
pick   (fork)

Page 84

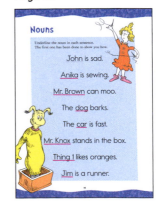

Parts of Speech

Have you heard about verbs?
Do you know about nouns?
They are some of the best
parts of speech that I've found!

Different types of words are known as
parts of speech.

Draw a line to match each word with its definition.

noun — a word that can be used to replace a noun
verb — a word that describes something
adjective — a person, place, or thing
pronoun — an action word

Page 86

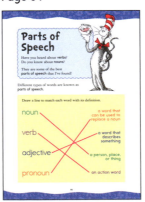

Nouns

Underline the noun in each sentence.
The first one has been done to show you how.

<u>John</u> is sad.

<u>Anika</u> is sewing.

<u>Mr. Brown</u> can moo.

The <u>dog</u> barks.

The <u>car</u> is fast.

<u>Mr. Knox</u> stands in the box.

<u>Thing 1</u> likes oranges.

<u>Jim</u> is a runner.

Circle the words that are nouns.

go (pig) bite
(boy) ride (tree)
(fox) (bike) hop
(man) bake (rug)

Write the words you circled.

boy	bike
fox	tree
man	rug
pig	

Verbs

Circle the words that are verbs.

(cry) cookie
(walk) (sit)
(skip) sad
hot apple

Choose one verb that you circled. Draw a picture showing that action.

Find and circle the verbs hidden among the letters.
Look for them up, down, across, and diagonally.
Use the words in the word box to help you.

run	eat	ski	read
jump	hide	clap	draw
play	ride	swim	nap

Y L U R M G I Y P V T
S D J I E S H (JUMP)
E L W D M Y I Z I Q V
A S I D K R P C E O R
T H X D U Y A L B K N
R G U O R U N A A D R
(R E A D) G A D P H Y
I X Z C Q W E O M Q O
L M B B D N O U P S N
(R I D E) M W S R A Q P
V N O B R Y W K N Y C
F X O W C T P G I V B

Adjectives

An adjective describes something.

Circle the words that are adjectives.

cat run
sad slide
(blue) (angry)
ham fish
(hot) (big)
(cold) apple
(wet) (hairy)

Find and circle the adjectives hidden among the letters.
Look for them up, down, across, and diagonally.
Use the words in the word box to help you.

happy	fun	tall	kind
clean	big	short	silly
red	small	good	wild

H T R R Q N I Y S D R
P A A Y W A J F M N Q
G L P L V E S O A I K
L O I P L L P D L L L
T X O Z Y C E Y L Y H
E C U D Q R L C J M X
O R V Y I L B U H U W
(W I L D) I R D I I S A
G O A S Z O L M G Y Q
G P M F S C Z P I E N
H V Z C J Q (S H O R T)
N O R S G (F U N) F F G

Pronouns

A pronoun is a word that replaces a noun.

Circle the pronoun that correctly finishes each sentence.

(I) Me) see a bee.

(Us /(We)) ride our bikes.

What time will ((you)/ us)
go home?

((They)/ Them) went up a tree.

He stamped ((his)/ him)
feet on the ground.

((She)/ Her) used the paint.

Fill in each blank with a pronoun that could
replace each noun in red.

Sally (She) likes
to play.

The farmer has to feed
the chickens (them).

Thing 1 and Thing 2
(They) go down
the slide.

I hope that boy (he)
will not fall.

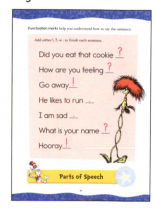

Punctuation marks help you understand how to say the sentence.

Add either !, ?, . to finish each sentence.

Did you eat that cookie ?

How are you feeling ?

Go away !

He likes to run .

I am sad .

What is your name ?

Hooray !

Parts of Speech

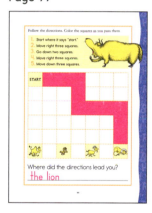

Follow the directions. Color the squares as you pass them.

1. Start where it says "start."
2. Move right three squares.
3. Go down two squares.
4. Move right three squares.
5. Move down three squares.

START

Where did the directions lead you?
the lion

Categories

Write each word in the correct box.

plane bike apple
spoon carrot car
fork egg plate

things you can eat	things you can eat with	things you can ride
apple	spoon	plane
carrot	fork	bike
egg	plate	car

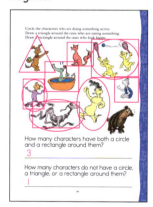

Circle the characters who are doing something active.
Draw a triangle around the ones who are eating something.
Draw a rectangle around the ones who look happy.

How many characters have both a circle
and a rectangle around them?
3

How many characters do not have a circle,
a triangle, or a rectangle around them?
1

Real or Imagined?

A sentence which states something that's true is a fact.
Something you believe is an opinion.
Circle whether each sentence is a fact or an opinion.

She has a blue dress. fact (opinion)

This cake is the best! fact (opinion)

The flower smells bad. fact (opinion)

I ate a red apple. (fact) opinion

It is 30 degrees today! (fact) opinion

They are running. (fact) opinion

The Grinch has a
very creepy smile. fact (opinion)

Nonfiction writing is about real people, places, events, or things.
Fiction is a story that is made up.

Draw a line to match the type of writing to
the description.

fiction

nonfiction

- a talking dog saves the day
- what I saw on my way to school
- a family of monsters lives under the bed
- how to plant a backyard garden

Reading Comprehension

Telling a Story

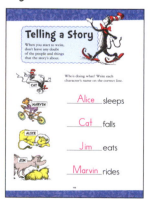

When you start to write,
don't leave any doubt
of the people and things
that the story's about.

Who's doing what? Write each
character's name on the correct line.

CAT

MARVIN

ALICE

JIM

Alice sleeps

Cat falls

Jim eats

Marvin rides

Unscramble the sentences and rewrite them so that
they make sense.

the bed. sleeps He in
He sleeps in the bed.

ice cream. loves He
He loves ice cream.

the flower. She smells
She smells the flower.

She car. the drives
She drives the car.

Numbers and Place Value

Numbers are very
important to know.
Let's count up to fifty.
Get ready, set, go!

Write the number that comes
before and after each number.
The first one has been done to
show you how.

11	12	13

76	23	78
15	16	17
42	43	44

34	35	36
8	9	10
26	27	28

Page 119

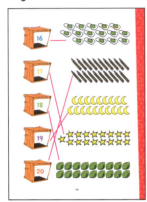

Page 120
Numbers 1 to 10
Write the number of fish for each dish.

Page 121
Write the number of stars in each group.
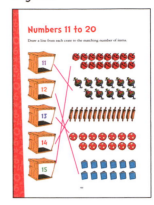

Page 122
Numbers 11 to 20
Draw a line from each crate to the matching number of items.
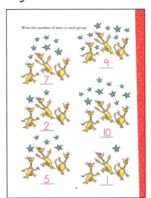

Page 123
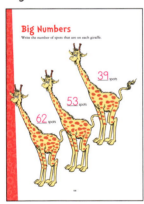

Page 125
Connect the dots from 1 to 30.
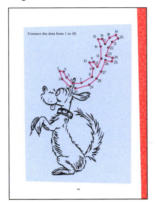

Page 126
Larger Numbers
Write the number that comes before and after each one.
The first one has been done to show you how.

Page 127
Fill in all the missing numbers on this grid.
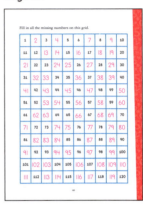

Page 128
Big Numbers
Write the number of spots that are on each giraffe.
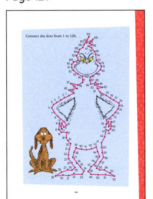

Page 129
Connect the dots from 1 to 120.
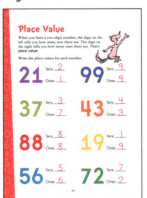

Page 130
Place Value
When you have a two-digit number, the digit on the left tells you how many tens there are. The digit on the right tells you how many ones there are. That's place value!
Write the place values for each number.
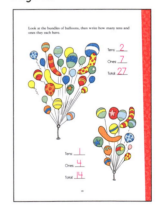

Page 131
Look at the bundles of balloons, then write how many tens and ones they each have.

Page 132
Place Value to Hundreds
Write the number of hundreds, tens, and ones under each number.
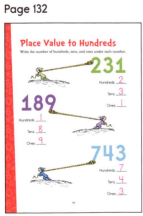

Page 133
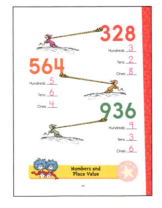
Numbers and Place Value

Page 137

Page 138
Skip Counting by Fives
How many books are in each of these bookcases?
Count by fives and write the number next to each one.

Page 139
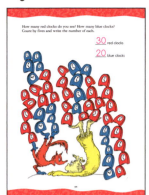
How many red clocks do you see? How many blue clocks?
Count by fives and write the number of each.

30 red clocks
20 blue clocks

Page 140

Skip Counting by Twos
Skip counting is when you count up by two, three, four, or more and skip numbers in between.

Count by two! Two, four, six, eight, ten, and keep going. When you reach the end, write the total. The first one has been done to show you how.

Total 8
Total 12
Total 6
Total 18

Page 141
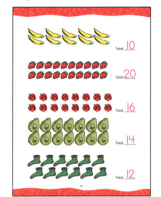
Total 10
Total 20
Total 16
Total 14
Total 12

Page 142
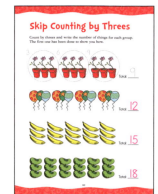
Skip Counting by Threes
Count by threes and write the number of things for each group. The first one has been done to show you how.

Total 9
Total 12
Total 15
Total 18

Page 143

Total 6
Total 21
Total 24
Total 9
Total 15

Page 144

Skip Counting by Fours
Count by fours and write the number of apples on each tree.

12 apples
8 apples
16 apples

Page 145
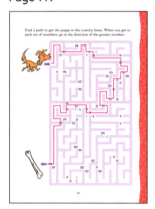
Count by fours to get to the end of the maze.

Skip Counting

Page 146
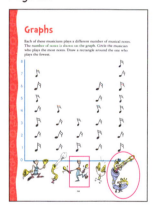
Exploring Values
When you learn about numbers, then, sooner or later, you should know which are less than and which ones are greater.

We use the symbols > and < to compare numbers and show when a number is greater than or less than the number that follows. We can also use the equals sign (=) to show that the number is equal to, or the same as, the other number.

It's easy to remember which symbol to use. The larger number is always on the wide, open side of the symbol, while the smaller number is always at the small, closed point. When the numbers are equal, the open space is the same on both sides!

Write either > (greater than), < (less than), or = (equal to) so that each statement is correct.

12 > 4   6 < 88

33 < 53   71 > 34

Page 147
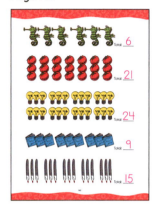
Write the number of feet below each thing. Then write either > (greater than) or < (less than) in between them.

2 < 6
8 > 4
6 > 2

Page 148

Greater Than, Less Than
Write either > (greater than), < (less than), or = (equal to) so that each statement is correct. The first one has been done to show you how.

5 + 10 > 12
8 + 4 < 21
3 + 9 < 13
6 + 3 = 9
11 + 4 > 7
7 + 3 < 12

Page 149

Find a path to get the puppy to the yummy bone. When you get to each set of numbers, go in the direction of the greater number.

Page 150
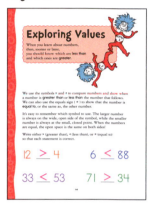
Graphs
Each of these musicians plays a different number of musical notes. The number of notes is shown on the graph. Circle the musician who plays the most notes. Draw a rectangle around the one who plays the fewest.

Page 151

Circle the fox with the most socks. Draw rectangles around the foxes that have the same number of socks.

Page 153

For every two-footed character you see, make a tally mark (|). Do the same for characters that have four feet and characters that have six feet.

2
4
6

Let's make a bar graph. Color one box for every tally mark you made.

2
4
6

How many have two feet? 9
How many have four feet? 2
How many have six feet? 1

Page 154
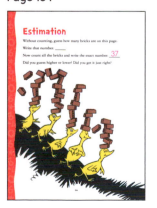
Estimation
Without counting, guess how many bricks are on this page.
Write that number. _____
Now count all the bricks and write the exact number. 37
Did you guess higher or lower? Did you get it just right?

Page 155
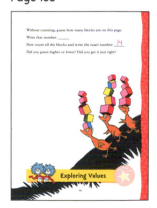
Without counting, guess how many blocks are on this page.
Write that number. _____
Now count all the blocks and write the exact number. 14
Did you guess higher or lower? Did you get it just right?

Exploring Values

Page 158

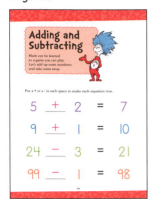

Adding and Subtracting

Math can be learned as a game you can play. Let's add up some numbers and take some away.

Put a + or a - in each space to make each equation true.

$5 + 2 = 7$

$9 + 1 = 10$

$24 - 3 = 21$

$99 - 1 = 98$

Page 159

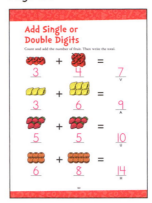

$4 + 4 = 8$

$15 - 5 = 10$

$8 - 8 = 0$

Color in all the spaces that equal exactly five.

2 + 4	11 - 6	9 - 3	2 + 3
10 - 2	2 + 2	4 + 1	9 - 4
14 - 4	12 - 7	4 + 3	13 - 5
3 + 2	10 - 4	5 + 0	4 + 2
10 - 6	1 + 4	3 - 2	10 - 5
2 + 2	16 - 6	15 - 10	6 + 2

Page 160

Add Single or Double Digits

Count and add the number of fruit. Then write the total.

$3 + 4 = 7$ V

$3 + 6 = 9$ A

$5 + 5 = 10$ U

$6 + 8 = 14$ H

Page 161

$10 + 3 = 13$ E

$3 + 12 = 15$ N

$6 + 11 = 17$ F

Reveal this message using the letter assigned to each answer.

$\underset{14}{H} \underset{9}{A} \underset{7}{V} \underset{13}{E} \quad \underset{17}{F} \underset{10}{U} \underset{15}{N}$

Page 162

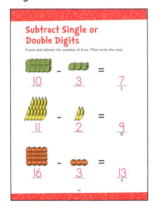

Subtract Single or Double Digits

Count and subtract the number of fruit. Then write the total.

$10 - 3 = 7$ I

$11 - 2 = 9$ O

$16 - 3 = 13$ Y

Page 163

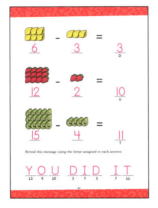

$6 - 3 = 3$ D

$12 - 2 = 10$ U

$15 - 4 = 11$ T

Reveal this message using the letter assigned to each answer.

$\underset{13}{Y} \underset{9}{O} \underset{10}{U} \quad \underset{3}{D} \underset{7}{I} \underset{11}{T}$ ... $\underset{7}{I} \underset{11}{T}$

Page 164

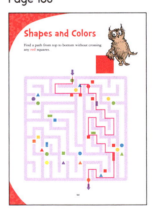

Add or Subtract Single Digits

Find a path from top to bottom. You can only move through a number that is exactly two more than the number you are on.

Page 165

Find a path from top to bottom. You can only move through a number that is exactly one less than the number you are on.

Adding and Subtracting

Page 166

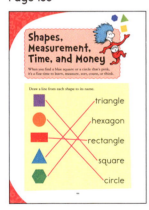

Shapes, Measurement, Time, and Money

When you find a blue square or a circle that's pink, it's a fine time to learn, measure, sort, count, or think.

Draw a line from each shape to its name.

- triangle
- hexagon
- rectangle
- square
- circle

Page 167

Find the hidden shapes in the picture and color them.
Color all the triangles blue. Color all the rectangles orange.
Color all the circles green.

Page 168

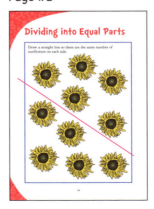

Shapes and Colors

Find a path from top to bottom without crossing any red squares.

Page 169

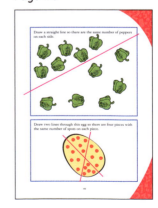

Find a path from top to bottom without crossing any orange circles.

Page 170

More Shapes and Colors

Using the guide at the bottom of this page, write a letter in each shape.

B U Z Z
B U Z Z
P O P
P O P

B O U P Z

Page 171

Using the guide at the bottom of this page, write a letter in each shape.

I CAN
MOO, CAN
YOU?

A C I M
N O U Y

Page 172

Dividing into Equal Parts

Draw a straight line so there are the same number of sunflowers on each side.

Page 173

Draw a straight line so there are the same number of peppers on each side.

Draw two lines through this egg so there are four pieces with the same number of spots on each piece.

Page 174

Page 175

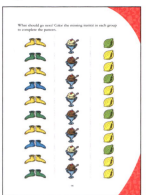

Page 176

Page 177

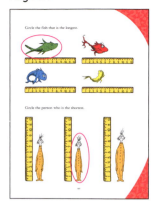

Page 178

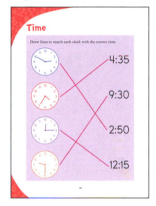

Page 179

Page 180

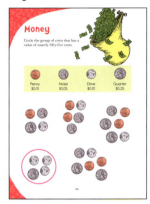

Page 181

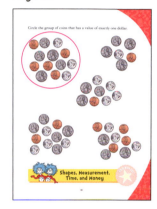

Page 186

Page 187

Page 189

Page 190

Page 196

Page 198

Page 200

Page 202

Page 208

The Things We All Need
Draw a line from the friend on the left to the friend on the right who can help.

Page 218

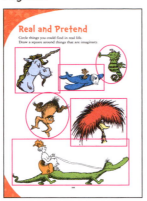

Real and Pretend
Circle things you could find in real life.
Draw a square around things that are imaginary.

Page 220

The Truth
Look at this scene. Circle **true** for the things that are true.
Circle **false** for the things that are not true.

The train is moving fast.	true	false
The trees are green.	true	false
Everybody is on the train.	true	false
The conductor is wearing a red hat.	true	false
The car is blue.	true	false
The car is on the ground.	true	false

Page 223

Help this bear find a path home.

Page 229

Unscramble the words to find ways people communicate.
Use the words in the word box to help you.

phone call | text | face to face | letter | email

letter — t r e l e t
email — m i l e a
phone call — h o e n p l a l c
text — x t t e
face to face — c f e a o t c f e a

Page 232

Face Your Fears
Oh no! This bear had a scary dream about losing his pants. Help him get through this maze of Snide bushes to find his pants and conquer his fears.

Page 238

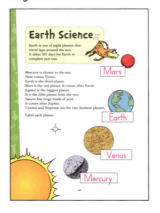

Earth Science
Earth is one of eight planets that travel laps around the sun. It takes 365 days for Earth to complete just one.

Mercury is closest to the sun.
Next comes Venus.
Earth is the third planet.
Mars is the red planet. It comes after Earth.
Jupiter is the biggest planet.
It is the fifth planet from the sun.
Saturn has rings made of acid.
It comes after Jupiter.
Uranus and Neptune are the two farthest planets.
Label each planet.

Mars
Earth
Venus
Mercury

Page 239

Neptune
Uranus
Saturn
Jupiter

What planet do we live on?
Earth

Page 240

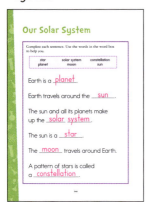

Our Solar System
Complete each sentence. Use the words in the word box to help you.

star | solar system | sun
planet | moon | constellation

Earth is a __planet__.
Earth travels around the __sun__.
The sun and all its planets make up the __solar system__.
The sun is a __star__.
The __moon__ travels around Earth.
A pattern of stars is called a __constellation__.

Page 242

Seasons of the Year
Match the season to its picture.

winter
spring
summer
autumn

What is another word for autumn?
fall

Page 243

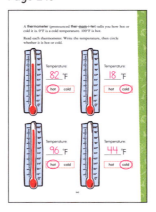

A thermometer (pronounced ther-mom-i-ter) tells you how hot or cold it is. 0°F is a cold temperature. 100°F is hot.

Read each thermometer. Write the temperature, then circle whether it is hot or cold.

Temperature: 82 °F hot / cold
Temperature: 18 °F hot / cold
Temperature: 96 °F hot / cold
Temperature: 44 °F hot / cold

Page 244

Weather
Match the weather word to its picture.

snow
wind
rain
sun
clouds

Page 246

Environments
When it's cold outside your home, it could be very hot somewhere else. The weather is different in different places all over the world.
Write two types of weather for each environment.

hot | wet | snowy
cold | dry | rainy

desert: hot / dry
arctic: cold / snowy
rainforest: wet / rainy

Page 247

Find and circle the weather words hidden among the letters. Look for them up, down, across, and diagonally.
Use the words in the word box to help you.

thunder | rain | sun
lightning | hail | storm
tornado | sleet | earthquake

R	A	H	B	U	Q	O	R	S	J	E
E	H	F	P	H	D	R	L	J	E	K
D	Z	A	R	A	D	A	I	G	V	A
N	C	A	N	P	O	N	U	H	A	U
U	W	R	W	R	N	U	S	T	S	Q
H	O	A	A	C	E	S	O	C	G	H
T	L	I	D	R	X	O	N	L	E	T
U	I	N	F	F	P	D	I	R	C	R
Y	Q	Q	V	R	A	A	N	E	W	A
S	T	O	R	M	H	Y	G	D	Y	E

Earth Science

Page 250

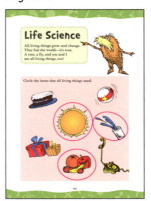

Life Science
All living things grow and change. They feel the world—it's true. A tree, a fly, and you and I are all living things, too!

Circle the items that all living things need.

Page 251

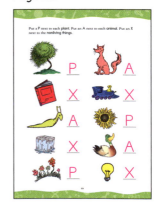

Put a P next to each **plant**. Put an A next to each **animal**. Put an X next to the **nonliving** things.

P A
X X
A P
X A
P X

302

Page 252

Plants

Label the parts of a plant.

| roots | stem | leaf | flower |

flower
stem
leaf
roots

Draw a seed. | Draw a plant. | Draw a tomato.

Page 253

A **fruit** grows on a tree or vine. It has seeds inside.
A **vegetable** grows in the ground. You eat its stem, leaves, or roots.

Put an X in the box next to the correct description for each picture.

☐ fruit ☒ vegetable
☒ fruit ☐ vegetable
☒ fruit ☐ vegetable
☐ fruit ☒ vegetable
☒ fruit ☐ vegetable
☐ fruit ☒ vegetable

Page 254

Animals and Their Habitats

Read the directions in each box. Label each animal part or circle.
Use the words in the word box to help you.

| foot | wing | fur | fin |

Circle one part of the fish that helps it live in water.
fin

Circle one part of the mountain goat that helps it live in the mountains.
foot

Circle the part of the polar bear that helps it live in the snow.
fur

Circle the part of the bird that helps it fly.
wing

Page 255

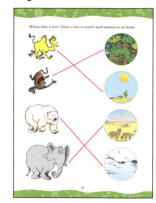

Where does it live? Draw a line to match each animal to its home.

Page 256

Parents and Babies

Match the animal parent to its baby.

Page 257

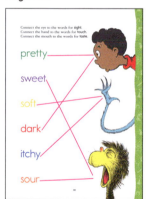

How do animal parents help their babies?
Connect the words to the pictures.

food

shelter

protection

What is another way animal parents help their babies?

teaching

Page 258

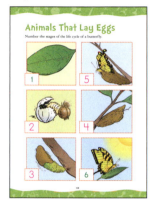

Animals That Lay Eggs

Number the stages of the life cycle of a butterfly.

1
5
2
4
3
6

Page 259

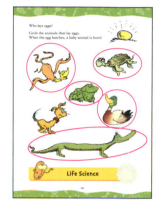

Who lays eggs?
Circle the animals that lay eggs.
When the egg hatches, a baby animal is born!

Life Science

Page 260

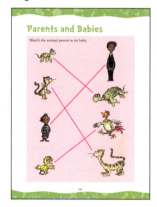

Health

Food and water, sleep and rest, hard work and time to play. These all help us stay healthy. We need them every day.

You have five senses that give you information about the world around you. Write the correct word to finish each sentence.

| ears | mouth | eyes | nose | hands |

I touch things with my **hands**
I smell things with my **nose**
I see things with my **eyes**
I taste things with my **mouth**
I hear things with my **ears**

Page 261

Connect the eye to the words for **sight**.
Connect the hand to the words for **touch**.
Connect the mouth to the words for **taste**.

pretty
sweet
soft
dark
itchy
sour

Page 262

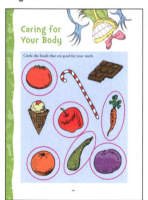

Caring for Your Body

Circle the foods that are good for your teeth.

Page 263

Write what each thing is used for.

keeping things clean
protect eyes from the sun
help stay above water
protect head if you fall
clean teeth and fresh breath
protect skin from the sun

Page 264

Healthy Foods

Eat healthy food to keep your body fueled up and ready to go!

Circle the foods you can eat that are good for you.
Put an X over the things that you cannot eat or drink.

whole-grain bread
fruit
oven mitt
vegetables
lightbulb
water

Page 266

Exercise

There are so many ways you can move your body and have fun.

Circle the things you can do that are good for you.
Put an X over images that do not show something healthy.

Page 268

Staying Safe

Circle the ones who are being safe.

Page 269

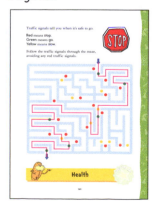

Traffic signals tell you when it's safe to go.

Red means stop.
Green means go.
Yellow means slow.

Follow the traffic signals through the maze, avoiding any red traffic signals.

Health

Page 270

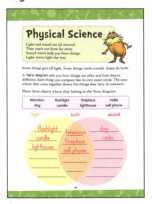

Physical Science

Light and sound are all around.
They reach out from far away.
Sound waves help you hear things.
Light waves light the way.

Some things give off light. Some things make sounds. Some do both.

A Venn diagram tells you how things are alike and how they're different. Each thing you compare has its own outer circle. The area where they come together shows the things they have in common.

Place these objects where they belong in the Venn diagram.

| television | flashlight | fireplace | radio |
| dog | candle | lighthouse | cell phone |

light   both   sound

flashlight, candle, lighthouse | television, fireplace, cell phone | dog, radio

---

Page 272

Light

Light comes from distant places, like a lamp or the sun.
When light shines on something, it becomes lighter.
When something is in the way, it makes a shadow.

The tree is in between the sun and the ground. Look at the tree's shadow on the ground.

Draw the object's shadow.

Page 273

Match the pictures to their shadows.

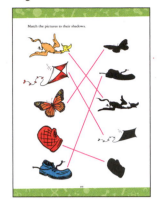

Page 274

Sound

Things that are close sound louder than things that are far away.
Circle the person who sounds louder.

If you yell, will your voice get louder or softer?
louder

When you whisper, does your voice sound louder or softer?
softer

Page 275

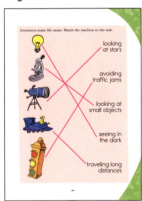

Loud or soft?
Sort these sounds into the correct box.

| cat purring | band | bird chirping | concert |
| fire truck | whistle | whisper | baby crying |

loud	soft
fire truck	cat purring
band	bird chirping
whistle	whisper
concert	
baby crying	

Page 276

Properties

Matter is anything that has weight and takes up space.

We use scientific words to describe how things look and feel.

Sort the words into the box that tells what they describe.

circle	green
blue	thin
soft	square
big	bumpy
triangle	red
small	hard

size	color
big	blue
small	green
thin	red

shape	texture
circle	soft
triangle	bumpy
square	hard

Page 278

Matter

Matter can be solid, liquid, or gas.

Complete the sentences with one of the three types of matter.

Water takes the shape of whatever you put it in. It is a **liquid**.

When water is frozen, it turns to ice. Ice is a **solid**.

When water is very hot, it turns to steam. Steam is a **gas**.

Snow is a **solid**.

Rain is a **liquid**.

Page 279

Label the pictures solid, liquid, or gas.

solid   solid
solid   gas
gas   liquid

Physical Science

Page 281

Inventions make life easier. Match the machine to the task.

looking at stars
avoiding traffic jams
looking at small objects
seeing in the dark
traveling long distances

Page 282

Scientific Process

Complete each sentence. Use the words in the word box to help you.

| test | share | imagine | |
| ask | write | create | scientific process |

When you do an experiment to explore a new idea, follow the steps in the **scientific** **process**.

Ask a question.

imagine what will happen,

make a plan to **test** your guess.

create your experiment.

write down what happens,

and **share** what you learned.

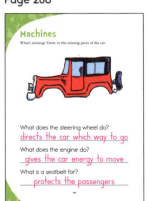

Page 283

A boat and a fork are both made of matter.
The boat is heavy, but the boat can float.
The fork is light, but it cannot float.

Some things push away the water. That makes them float. If something does not push away the water, it will sink.

Complete each sentence. Use the words in the word box to help you.

| sink | float | light | push | matter | pull |

Everything you can touch is made of **matter**.

When you use force to move a thing closer to you: **pull**

The opposite of pull: **push**

Go to the bottom: **sink**

Stay on top: **float**

The opposite of heavy: **light**

Page 284

Science Tools

Match the name to the science tool.

telescope
scale
measuring cup
pencil
calculator
magnet

Page 285

Find and circle the science terms hidden among the letters. Look for them up, down, across, and diagonally. Use the words in the word box to help you.

| float | matter | question | sound | energy |
| sink | experiment | process | light | invention |

H	M	L	D	A	T	R	S	Q	I	E
E	B	H	C	E	I	J	P	L	N	Q
T	D	I	E	N	T	T	F	U	V	R
N	E	G	S	E	I	T	S	B	E	N
E	I	H	N	R	H	E	D	I	N	P
M	O	A	O	G	Y	N	C	T	I	R
I	R	D	I	Y	U	F	A	W	I	O
R	E	A	T	O	V	L	R	A	O	C
E	N	U	A	S	S	E	O	S	T	E
P	A	K	E	A	P	A	O	I	D	S
X	H	T	U	L	R	T	E	R	N	S
E	N	U	Q	M	A	T	T	E	R	K

Page 286

Machines

What's missing? Draw in the missing parts of the car.

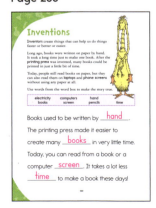

What does the steering wheel do?
directs the car which way to go

What does the engine do?
gives the car energy to move

What is a seatbelt for?
protects the passengers

Page 287

Label the parts of the computer.

| mouse | keyboard | screen |

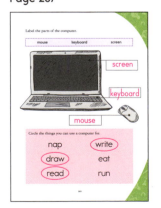

screen
keyboard
mouse

Circle the things you can use a computer for.

nap   (write)
(draw)   eat
(read)   run

Page 288

Inventions

Inventors create things that can help us do things faster or better or easier.

Long ago, books were written on paper by hand. It took a long time just to make one book. After the printing press was invented, many books could be printed in just a little bit of time.

Today, people still read books on paper, but they can also read them on laptops and phone screens without using any paper at all.

Use words from the word box to make the story true.

| electricity | computers | hand | |
| books | screen | pencil | time |

Books used to be written by **hand**.

The printing press made it easier to create many **books** in very little time.

Today, you can read from a book or a computer **screen**. It takes a lot less **time** to make a book these days!